INSIDE ONE
AUTHOR'S HEART

A Deeply Personal Sharing
with My Readers

Also by Eugenia Price

FICTION

St. Simons Trilogy

Lighthouse
New Moon Rising
The Beloved Invader

Florida Trilogy

Don Juan McQueen
Maria
Margaret's Story

Savannah Quartet

Savannah
To See Your Face Again
Before the Darkness Falls
Stranger in Savannah

Georgia Trilogy

Bright Captivity

NONFICTION

Discoveries
The Burden Is Light
Early Will I Seek Thee
Share My Pleasant Stones
Woman to Woman
What Is God Like?
Beloved World
A Woman's Choice
God Speaks to Women Today
The Wider Place
Make Love Your Aim
Just as I Am

Learning to Live from the Gospels
The Unique World of Women
Learning to Live from the Acts
St. Simons Memoir
Leave Yourself Alone
Diary of a Novel
No Pat Answers
Getting Through the Night
What Really Matters
Another Day
At Home on St. Simons

INSIDE ONE AUTHOR'S HEART

A Deeply Personal Sharing
with My Readers

EUGENIA PRICE

TURNER

PUBLISHING COMPANY

From my heart, to my readers
everywhere, who will understand,
I'm sure, that I cannot work hard
on the remaining two novels in the
Georgia Trilogy and also take time
and energy for personal autographs.

With my love and gratitude to each
of you.

Turner Publishing Company

Nashville, Tennessee

www.turnerpublishing.com

Cover design: Bruce Gore

Library of Congress Cataloging-in-Publication Data Upon Request

9781684427451   Paperback
9781684427468   Hardback
9781684427475   eBook

Printed in the United States of America

17 18 19 20 10 9 8 7 6 5 4 3 2 1

CONTENTS

INTRODUCTION

In chapter 1 you will find *my* version of what took place on St. Simons Island, Georgia, on May 4 of the year 1991, when Doubleday, my publisher, celebrated the publication of *Bright Captivity* and my seventy-fifth birthday. But this book is also about much more. After all, years may have passed by the time you open it. Telling you about that unforgettable day is important because it was then that I first felt that I had to write this book.

In the other chapters I have tried to pay sincere tribute to you, my faithful readers who have stayed beside me throughout my long writing life, by letting you into my world. Not long ago one reader said, "Genie, we all feel as though we know you, but how we wish we knew you better. Knew more of what you think and how you live, because even between books you stay such a part of our lives." In these pages I have simply tried to share *myself*. To give you, whose affection and loyalty and prayers have sustained me, a deeply personal idea of what this writer's life is like. I have also attempted to respond to a few of the questions you've asked most often.

Some may think the effort too sentimental, even arrogant, on my part. So be it. For me, the writing has been a tough exercise in humility—at least as I understand its meaning. No one could deserve the kind of devotion you continue to give me, but you do go on giving it. This little book is between us. It is for you who read, from the heart of this author who writes—not always superbly, by any means, but always up to the very best she can do. I have been told that the special, lasting bond that seems uniquely ours is rare. Experienced book people who know have told me that again and again. So, at age seventy-five, which is supposed to be a kind of milepost, I really had no choice but to try to let you know the deep value to me of that bond.

PART I

1

My Big Day on
St. Simon's Island

F ew can boast of a driver with a Ph.D. I can. At least I could on the perfect sunny morning of May 4, 1991, when Dr. Jimmy Humphlett, on orders from his wife, Eileen, my assistant, rolled up our lane a few minutes after nine. Jimmy was his usual attentive, charming, humorous self, but he made no bones about "operating fully under orders." Eileen's orders. Eileen wasn't along and I knew that she, Ellen Archer, my publicist, and Jayne Schorn, my publisher's marketing director, were already down at the new Island bandstand—in charge. For six weeks or more, Eileen and Joyce Blackburn, my best friend, had worked with Millie Wilcox and Woody Woodside, of both the St. Simons and Brunswick Chambers of Commerce, making mysterious "plans and arrangements," one of which plainly was that Dr. Jimmy would be in charge of me for the day.

Someone certainly needed to be! My own inner thoughts

13

as we drove down sun-shot Frederica Road that morning were a jumble—tingles of excitement and tingles of nerves. Although I'd been busy with a hectic interview schedule for over a month, I still knew something of what was planned. But Joyce, Eileen, and (by long distance from New York) Ellen had been at the helm of what was being called—thanks to my friend Zell Miller, Georgia's governor—Eugenia Price Day in Georgia. Heaven knows, public appearances are not new to me. This one was different. I live here. Most of the time I'm part of the scenery. Would people really come out to stand in the already warming Georgia sun so early on a Saturday morning? I knew that Doubleday, the sponsor of the Day, had arranged (through Eileen, of course) for a great jazz combo, the Ben Tucker Quartet from Savannah. Music would help, but if I fell silent for part of the drive down Frederica Road, it was because my insides were churning and I was already bone- tired. (After all these years of hard work, feeling tired still always surprises me.)

In addition to all the radio, press, and television interviews I had done during the month past to discuss my new novel, *Bright Captivity*, I had signed my name more than four thousand times in area stores and on labels to be pasted in the book. So I not only was a bit frayed but realized suddenly that I had almost no idea of *exactly* what was going to take place. I seemed sure only that some of my loyal readers would turn up and that I had selected slacks and a blouse that would withstand wrinkles as I moved through whatever lay ahead. Thanks to my friends on neighboring Sea Island, where the famous Cloister Hotel is located, there would be a booksellers' luncheon and then autographing at the St. Simons Island Club. I was no longer doing signing parties in stores, but I'd have a chance to meet and say a few words to at least some of those great readers I'd counted on through the long years. But would people really come to the bandstand for what was being called a Public Tribute to me that morning?

"Eileen will be there waiting," Joyce said, knowing that always comforted me.

"I hope so," I mumbled.

Of course, she was waiting when Jimmy pulled into the designated parking spot. I was sure Eileen would introduce me to the local and state officials who had honored me by coming. Actually, I felt almost sorry for them and wondered if, as politicians, they'd really had much choice in the matter. When someone has been trapped into appearing in public as often as I have, this question does come to mind. My favorite of all United States senators, Georgia's Wyche Fowler, had told me in a long-distance call that although he had other commitments, he was sending someone from his Washington office. Georgia's Senator Sam Nunn and Representative Lindsay Thomas would send messages.

My heart was already overflowing from the wonderfully intimate, deliciously catered dinner party Joyce had given me the evening before at Eileen's house, where only those in my close personal circle were present: Carolyn Blakemore, my editor; Lila Karpf, my agent; Ellen Archer and Jayne Schorn; Bebe Cole from Doubleday's sales department; Nancy Goshorn, my researcher; my fellow novelist Tina McElroy Ansa; and Sarah Bell Edmond, who takes care of my house.

Emotion almost overcame me as we drove up behind the bandstand that morning into what appeared to be a veritable throng of people, all smiling, all waving, all welcoming me. It's a bit of a blur now, but I remember

Eileen hugged me first thing and asked if I was all right, and I remember her saying that my longtime friend Woody Woodside would lead the Pledge of Allegiance. (I still get a special kind of historical novelist's thrill when Southerners insist on pledging allegiance to the Union flag!)

From behind the bandstand platform, I could hear that great jazz beat. After Eileen made the introductions to officials I didn't already know, the combo struck up "When the Saints Go Marching In"—and in I marched. One photo shows that I did a few dance steps and then stood looking out over the crowd. Yes. There was a crowd! Estimates vary, but there were literally hundreds of persons standing out there. In the front row of chairs set up just below the bandstand sat most of my special people—my dear ones from New York, everyone who had been at Joyce's elegant dinner the evening before, and old Island friends. If I'd ever wondered how Eileen and Company could bring off this celebration, I knew beyond a doubt when the attractively printed program listing all the welcomings and tributes to be made, the citations to be given me by the local and state brass, was followed to a tee. (Eileen is a born producer!) Maybe you don't believe politicians can be brief, eloquent, and to the point, but Georgia politicians and officials can be. All who paid a tribute or gave me a gift or a framed citation warmed my heart still more by their evident sincerity and good will toward me. And when, at my request, Stan Moran, with his beautiful voice, sang my favorite song, "Battle Hymn of the Republic," there were tears in my eyes, and I don't tear easily.

Best of all, there before me were hundreds of my readers! I kept waving and blowing kisses. So did they. I had exerted enough influence on the day's plans so that in lieu of birthday "gifts" to me, it had been requested that contributions be sent to Habitat for Humanity. A portion of the profits from book sales that day were also being given to Habitat and to the St. Simons Museum of Coastal History. About halfway through the program, which moved along at a swift, happy clip, Eileen pointed out Tom and Dianne Hall, who had honored me by driving down from Habitat headquarters in Americus, Georgia.

Doubleday and my loving St. Simons Island friends had thought up E. P. Day to celebrate my seventy-fifth birthday and the publication of *Bright Captivity*, the first novel in my planned Georgia Trilogy. Sitting there on the platform that day, I wondered how I'd ever be able to thank God that I could earn my living by writing books. Then I heard State Representative Willou Smith reading Governor Zell Miller's proclamation. Next, while I was still thinking about my inadequate gratitude, there was a loud wave o f merry laughter. Reading another proclamation from Governor Miller, State Representative Ron Fennel had just announced that the gover.nor had appointed me a lieutenant colonel in the Georgia State Militia. I'm as antimilitary as they come and no one laughed as hard as I. Thank you, Governor Miller—*I think*.

By then, I was relaxed and enjoying myself because no one could possibly doubt that love reigned everywhere. The air vibrated with it. Love enfolded and inspired me during those now unforgettable moments following Joyce Blackburn's free, encompassing, and altogether graceful introduction of the "character" named Eugenia Price, with whom Joyce lives her life and with whom she too first found St. Simons Island some thirty years ago. I got to my feet, but I could do nothing except stand there beside Joyce; the waves of applause made music for me because I knew everyone was also applauding her. One of the best things about living on St. Simons is that she and I have been almost like one person to our friends and neighbors and readers. Plainly we still were as we stood there on that bright, bright May morning.

As the cheering and applause went on, the long years during which I've been sitting at this old manual typewriter telescoped in my mind. I honestly don't remember, but I was probably applauding all of you, too, because no one knows better than I that I would not have been there without each of you who read my books. You may not actually have been with us that enchanted morning, but you helped make it all happen.

Once I began to speak from my heart to those who were there, I knew as surely as I'd ever known anything that I *had* to write this book. Hearing myself say that I would do just that—that I intended to do it even before I went back to work on the second novel in the Georgia Trilogy—surprised me as much as it surprised my listeners. I know I surprised Joyce, Eileen, Ellen Archer, and Jayne Schorn. Ellen and Jayne and Nancy Goshorn, who does my research, were sitting in the front row near Carolyn, my editor, and Lila, my agent. I saw how stunned they all were.

Mildred Huie, our enduring friend and a famous St. Simons artist, put those morning festivities in her usual striking perspective: "Genie, even on St. Simons, that many people together would have produced bickering of some kind—hurt feelings about something. Not today! You may be the only person who could have brought us all together in an atmosphere of that kind of love."

I don't know that I agree with Mildred that no one else could have done it. I only know that the atmosphere of love was there—everywhere. The breathtakingly beautiful bouquet of fragrant white roses Millie Wilcox handed me from the Brunswick and St. Simons Chambers of Commerce has faded now, but not my overwhelmingly vivid memories—even of the final moments as I made my way offstage, stopping for one more picture, one more hug, one more greeting, back to Jimmy's car. The good beat of "Saints" is still ringing in my ears.

Eileen's next order to Jimmy was "to the Island Club!" My bookseller friends, as loyal as are my readers, had come from all around the area to be with me at the luncheon hosted by the elegant St. Simons Island Club. After we talked and ate, I spoke for a few minutes to the booksellers. Then Eileen took my hand again to lead me to the autographing table, where a long, long line of readers was already waiting, some with armfuls of *Bright Captivity*.

From that moment until after five in the afternoon, I signed books. If you were there, you know a lot more than I about the excitement: the unveiling by Millie Wilcox of Pamela Patrick's gorgeous painting for the jacket of *Bright Captivity*, the huge birthday cake, a veritable masterpiece by Sea Island's pastry chef (he reproduced the entire book jacket in the icing). You heard a lot more of talented Marge Kelso's piano than I was able to hear from the adjoining parlor. You also know, or witnessed what I've only been told, about the long, long, long lines of people who stood waiting outside—all the way to the parking lot—for my scribble. If you were in that line, maybe you were even fortunate enough to have been served the club's refreshing lemonade by Ann Heins and her staff with the help of my friend Amanda Borders and my Southeastern sales rep, Michael Coe, both of whom I barely had a chance to see.

The very fact that I was too busy autographing to know much of what went on made me even more determined to write this book. Because you who were there were a part of so much I *didn't* experience, I at least want you to know something of how it all affected me.

One of the reasons I've had to call a halt to any more parties in bookstores across the country is that they seem never to last the one or two scheduled hours. Nor did this one. It was supposed to be over at 3 P.M. I left the Island Club well after five, with barely enough time for Jimmy to drive Joyce and me to our house so that we could show Steve Rubin our place in the woods. You see, Steve, the president and publisher of Double.day, had endured plane delays all the way from New York to Brunswick. I was upset that he'd missed most of the day because I love him and so wanted him to meet you, my readers. But he scarcely made it for the evening and I scarcely had time for a quick shower and a change of clothes before the dinner Steve was hosting that night at my friend Alfonza Ramsey's restaurant, the Old Plantation Supper Club. I did, however, have time to show Steve the handmade "gathering" basket a reader had given me—by then filled with notes, letters, cards, gifts of all kinds, including a child's impressive rendition of the *Bright Captivity* Jacket design. To this day I'm frustrated because the drawing is signed only "Joanna," and I have no idea how to thank her except here. Thank you, Joanna, and I did have a chance that evening to show my publisher your beautiful artwork.

Within the hour, at Alfonza's restaurant, after master of ceremonies Fred Bentley had introduced Steve to our hundred or so dinner guests, no one would have guessed that Steve hadn't been with us all through the day. My longing for him to be exposed to the kind of devotion my readers continue to shower on me seemed suddenly foolish. *He knew.* Steve Rubin can't help being a fine publisher because his warm, open, intelligent mind can encompass all kinds of people.

On his feet as host, welcoming the dinner guests, Steve not only made us all laugh by saying he'd found from experience that it's wise to take *my* publishing suggestions; the very tone of what he said and the way he said it let me know that in all ways where you, my readers, and I are concerned, *he is with us.* He's amazed but believes me when I tell him that you actually ask me to thank Doubleday for publishing the kind of books I write!

After Steve made me proud in his welcoming speech, gentle, articulate Fred Bentley took over. Fred is a prominent Marietta, Georgia, attorney, art and book collector, but mainly *my friend.* With his usual finesse and charm, Fred introduced the seven novel dedicatees present: Jo Couper Cauthorn, to whom I dedicated *Bright Captivity*, Dena Snodgrass, *Margaret's Story*, Nancy Goshorn, *Maria*, Marion Hemperley, *To See Your Face Again*, Barbara Bennett, *Before the Darkness Falls*, Eileen Humphlett, *Stranger in Savannah*, and Joyce Blackburn, *The Beloved Invader.*

Then there were numerous toasts, and near the end of dinner (skillfully supervised by Alfonza Ramsey and Emma Gibson), Fred flashed his disarming smile and began to present the "surprise" entertainment that had been planned without my knowledge by Joyce and Eileen. A characteristic "Genie Price" dinner program, which I hadn't seen before, had been printed. I was dumbfounded and delighted to read *Politics, Books,* and *Inspiration.* With a rush of emotion and anticipation, I saw the "acts" Fred was introducing—

and what acts! No wonder I'm never bored with either Joyce or Eileen. Their capacity for variety is endless. Seeing the heading *Politics*, I could only think, "Uh-oh!" Most who know me know I'm a convinced, though currently out-of-style, liberal. (There are still a McGovern button, a Carter-Mondale button, a Harkin- for-Senate button, and a Mondale-Ferraro button pinned to the grass cloth of our dressing room!) So, when I saw the name of one of my favorite, far-out, truly funny friends. National Democratic Committee member Juanelle Edwards, I thought I couldn't wait until she was on her feet. That night Juanelle outdid even herself. I laughed until my face hurt, although the only line I remember now, amid peals of laughter from my tolerant conservative friends as well as from us liberals, is Juanelle's declaring that "Eugenia Price has written more books than Ronald Reagan ever read!"

When the laughter and applause for Juanelle finally faded, up jumped a solidly bipartisan duo, both my good friends. State Representative Willou Smith, a Republican, and Mary Hitt, formerly the Democratic mayor of Jesup, Georgia, and once a strong Democratic candidate for lieutenant governor of the state. Doffing straw boaters and dressed in red, white, and blue, those two gorgeous gals flipped us all with a wild, high-kicking performance of the old song "Friendship." Not all of us agree in Georgia, but we do just fine together, thank you.

I had already seen on the program that another cherished friend, Marion Connor Price, would be doing one of her famous interpretative readings, but until I saw her name, I hadn't even known Marion was in the crowded dining room. For years she has been rewriting dramatically brilliant versions of my long novels, then performing them as mono-dramas before packed houses up and down the coast. It didn't take me long to realize that beautiful Marion would be doing something that night from *Bright Captivity*. When Fred introduced her, she hurried from her place several tables away, gave me a warm hug, and began her monologue, in costume, as the Scottish housekeeper Anne Couper Fraser had come to love during the time she and her husband, John, lived in the Fraser home near London's Portman Square. Even the waiters slowed to listen, and I sat there, once again amazed by those interpretative skills. For several magic moments, in a surprisingly quiet dining room, Marion was my character Flora McLeod.

I was having the time of my life, but even in all the excitement, I realized I had seldom been so tired. Occasional bites of Alfonza's superb steak were sustaining me. But by the time my tender, loving friend Elizabeth Harris, Georgia's First Lady for eight years and one of my most loyal and encouraging readers, got to her feet for the act called *Inspiration*, I was glad and relieved because I knew Elizabeth had already prayed for me to make it without running entirely out of energy. After all, she knew I had been signing, talking, hugging, and laughing all day in addition to speaking at the morning festivities and again at the booksellers' luncheon— and according to my program, would also be speaking after Elizabeth's beautiful words. Fred Bentley would be introducing me again and I would have to think of something to say. My heart brimmed, but literally, I could feel my energy draining away. A glance at where my wonderful doctor. Bill Hitt, was sitting, just below the speakers' table, reassured me. Bill was keeping an eye on me—had been all day. I knew because I'd seen him everywhere. Not because I was ill in any special way, but because I was almost seventy-five, and if anyone knew I hadn't slowed down since early morning. Bill did.

He and I exchanged smiles while lovely Elizabeth Harris was saying the things only Elizabeth could say about my faith, what my inspirational books had meant to her and her family through the years, how she'd loved attending my autograph-ing parties for the novels at Rich's in Atlanta in the old days. No other person, certainly no one as busy and in demand, had been more of a booster than Elizabeth was while she was First Lady of Georgia. Her closing remarks were far more than "inspirational" to me. Her great heart and her faith melded into mine during those closing moments, and I began to regain my strength. Strength enough to get to my feet when Fred said it was time. I only remember saying, "I've never been this happy in my long, mostly happy, life!" Joyce tells me I said a few other things, but I must have looked drained, which was exactly the way I felt. I know I did, because people didn't rush up to me— even after we all sang my favorite hymn, "Amazing Grace." They just stood there applauding again, waving, blowing kisses, and clearing the way for Jimmy Humphlett to propel me out to his waiting car.

Then Joyce and I were at home and I was in bed within minutes. I fell asleep almost at once, but not without a final thought: I *have* to write a little book to tell my readers who weren't with me in person at least something about My Day.

I've tried here, however inadequately, to do that.

2

The Bond Between Us

The days that came after the Big Day on May 4, 1991, took on a glow all their own. For the remainder of that month my time was spent opening, reading, marveling at, and trying to give thanks for the stacks of mail— letters, cards, gifts, telegrams—that kept coming, along with the inevitable phone calls from friends near and far who had been on St. Simons Island that day or for one reason or another couldn't make it. Evidently I wasn't the only one with glowing memories. I heard from hundreds o f you who had come to St. Simons to be with me for the celebration. I'm glad I did, since for me the entire Day whirled past with scarcely time to do more than hug, smile, try to show my heart. One person can take in only so much, and I did, I'm told, sign well over a thousand books. Those of you who called or wrote to tell me how much downright fun you'd had, especially those who sent funny and happy pictures of the Day, helped me put some of it together, but I know I missed a lot.

One call I hurried to make was to my longtime friend Faith Brunson, for years the book buyer supreme in Atlanta, at Rich's well-known department store. She had injured her leg and couldn't make it down for my celebration. Even before I called to thank those who had done so much to make the Day memorable, I made contact with Faith.

For over twenty-five years Faith has been not only my friend but my sounding board when I have a decision to make about which book to write or which way to turn in whatever publishing problem I face. For far longer, she was one of the best-known, most successful book buyers in the United States. Most of the knowledgeable authors in the country hastened to do a party at Rich's if Faith Brunson beckoned. Of course, I was among them. I needed to tell Faith that somehow Eugenia Price Day had filled me with a new kind of awed astonishment at the loyalty of my readers.

During the many interviews I did on behalf of *Bright Captivity*, I had been asked over and over what accounted for such loyalty. Faith knew the answer.

"Genie, the kind of relationship you have with your readers won't happen again—ever." When I asked why, she answered, "Because the world is changing and that means people are changing too. I know other authors with faithful followings, but none quite like yours."

Faith had been right beside me as a volunteer only two weeks earlier at the Book Festival for Literacy in Atlanta—on a cold, windy, rainy day under a big white tent. For hours I'd signed *Bright Captivity* and talked with readers who not only braved the chilly elements but, under umbrellas much of the time, had enjoyed one another's company. Faith reminded me of that festival day plus the many years at Rich's when people had sometimes stood in line for hours, chatting, discussing various characters in my novels, comparing favorite titles. "The thousands of people who love the way you write," Faith went on, "also love each other! I well remember how few complaints we had in the old days at Rich's when they had to stand and stand in those long lines, because they liked being together with your books to share."

We talked for half an hour or so about everything that had happened during E. P. Day. Then I told her about that moment when, on my feet at the morning festivities on the bandstand. I'd surprised even myself by telling the crowd that I was going to try to show my gratitude to them by writing a short book about the mysterious bond my readers and I enjoy.

Without a moment's hesitation, she said, "Do it! Write that book. Those dear people all feel as though they know you. They deserve to know you better."

"You can guess what some of the establishment critics will say about such a book, can't you?" I asked.

"Of course I can guess, but who cares? You're the one who knows your readers and they'll love it! What difference does it make what the critics say? Most of them don't know we're out here in the hinterlands anyway. Just write it from your heart."

"They'll say it's schmaltzy, dripping with sentiment." I laughed. "I guess it will be, but I'm going to do it. And hey, I think you've given me a title!"

Without missing a beat. Faith agreed that *Inside One Author's Heart* was just right. Finding *the* title is seldom easy. Not for me, at least, but I know this one says what I mean.

You and I do share an almost mystical bond, and if it sounds sentimental, so be it.

Many of you who had seen Joyce, Eileen, and me at the Book Festival in Atlanta just two weeks earlier had driven down to St. Simons for my Big Day. I honestly think seeing you again so soon gave me the inspiration and encouragement I needed to set aside the *Bright Captivity* sequel long enough to write this little book.

One of my most perceptive and loyal readers, Betty Lam-berth, was among those at the Book Festival. In the midst of the Island festivities on the morning of E. P. Day, I again spotted both Betty and her husband, James. Betty, once a college professor and now a high school teacher, addressed a letter, written as soon as they returned home, to Joyce and Eileen, too.

Dear Miss Genie, Joyce, and Eileen,
What a wonderful day May 4, 1991, was on St. Simons! And how special to see you ladies in April at the Book Festival, then again in May. I'm sure autographing parties are taxing, but you make a great team with Joyce talking with the people waiting in line, Eileen moving the herd along or opening books for Genie, and Miss Genie just looking sweet, calm, and delighted with us all while she *must* be suffering an Excedrin pain in her back, shoulders, and neck!

Correct about back, shoulders, and neck but not about always being "sweet" or "calm." Feeling delighted, yes. I live to write books. I am exhilarated when faced with a long line of readers. But I certainly don't always feel sweet or calm. This seems as good a time as any to admit that even a stack of heart-lifting letters like Betty Lamberth's can overwhelm me when the mail comes at the end of long hours of writing. Ask Joyce, who has learned exactly the safe way to smile when, after reading my mail for nearly an hour, I sometimes blurt: "If they like my books so well, why don't they leave me alone so I can write them? Today, everyone seems to want a favor of some kind!"

I am not always calm and sweet but I am always human, and once Joyce smiles indulgently, I find relief in laughing at myself because one thing is sure—I do stay grateful to you. For you. And you who read my books have taught me what must be the most important lesson of my entire life; *No author writes books for everyone.*

Those of you who write me of your impatience until the publication of my next novel already know that you are as different from one another as are wildflowers. We all are. Later in this book I mention reviewers and readers who are bored by what I write. For now, let the lesson I've learned become yours when for one reason or another you dislike a certain novel you happen to read. Don't blame the author or the publisher. No author writes books for everyone. We are all different. God did not pour the human race into one mold. Not all of us will like the same kind of characters, plots, settings.

Frankly, it's amazing to me that millions of you continue to prefer the kind of stories I choose to write, that your letters go on telling me of daily prayers for my health, that you make no bones about caring about me as a human being.

When I'm tired from a long day, this incredible caring

is a mystery to me, but it *is* the source of my strength. It makes me even more determined to go on writing for you. Why try to solve a mystery that does such wonders for me and seems also to bring happiness to you?

At best, isn't mystery an integral part of life?

3

1961: A New World

L ogic tells me that, of course, some things *are* accidents— good and bad. God does *not send* bad things. He is simply *in* everything with us—good and bad—as He said He would be. So, although finding St. Simons Island the way I found it with Joyce, back in the year 1961, may have seemed accidental, I wonder.

Promoting what was then a new book of mine, *Beloved World*, we "happened" to have spent Thanksgiving Day in Charleston, South Carolina, en route to Jacksonville, Florida, where my next autographing party was scheduled. We "happened" to be somewhat idly scanning an A A A road map when we spied a little island off the coast of Georgia called St. Simons. One of us "happened" to say that although we'd never spent any time in Georgia, the very name St. Simons sounded interesting. Then one of us flipped to the historical notes in the A A A TourBook and read a short paragraph about an Episcopal chapel called Christ Church, built in 1884 by a former New Yorker, Anson Greene Phelps Dodge, Jr., in memory of his bride, who had died on their honeymoon. Accident or not, we would spend our two free nights, before heading to Jackson.ville, on St. Simons Island. And without giving it another thought, we pointed my 1959 white Bonneville straight into a new world for us both. A whole new life.

Back then I was not new to the world of book publishing. I had already published some ten or twelve nonfiction titles but was definitely reawakening to my earlier goal of someday writing a novel. Joyce knew that had been an almost forgotten dream from my teens. I mentioned it, usually half kidding, but I'd brought it up often enough so that after we read that legend about Anson Dodge and Christ Church, she said in passing, "A good plot for a novel."

Yes.

I had held that dream lightly for years, even though I had never been, and still am not, a great novel reader. I strongly prefer biographies. I have simply wanted, since the age of sixteen or seventeen, to write novels, and for a reason I couldn't explain, I wanted to write novels about real people—people who had actually lived. I'd thought about the stories of various Bible characters, a subject publishers had suggested. Nothing sparked me much, though, and anyway I was busy most of the time autographing, filling speaking dates, answering mail, writing nonfiction books. In 1961 I was probably thinking "novel" again because *Beloved World*, the book Joyce and I were out promoting, was subtitled *The Story of God and People*. I was young enough in 1959 and 1960 to try to write (actually to connect) the whole story of the Bible using the form of a novel. A daring attempt, but

I must have done something right, because *Beloved World* has never been out of print in all these years and is now in a handsome trade paperback edition issued by Doubleday in May 1991.

Anyway, I was thinking "story" that day as we headed for St. Simons Island, never dreaming that the fragment about Anson Dodge and his little church at Frederica was about to turn into my first novel. *The Beloved Invader.* Of course, neither of us had the slightest notion that we would soon be meeting living descendants of people whose lives would so interest me, and that not one novel but a whole trilogy of novels would one day take shape. The St. Simons Trilogy was written in reverse order, by the way, because that was the sequence in which we found the research material. We had no inkling at all, meandering down the coast, how vastly our lives were about to change.

On the very first day we awakened on St. Simons Island, we drove immediately up Frederica Road to find the little church-yard, both of us somehow aware that something significant was about to take place. After all these years, I now seem almost able to see us standing halfway up the brick walk that leads to the tiny, elegant, white church—in almost transfixed silence. I remember that we rather sensed our way up the walk and around the small building as we headed for the cemetery that still shouts Eternity to us, almost as though we were moving under orders. What we meant to find neither of us knows to this day. Neither of us knew then. We thought we were simply experiencing together the eternal certainty of ongoing life in the shadow-and-sun-streaked churchyard at Frederica.

After a time Joyce said (she didn't ask, she said), "I think you're going to write a novel about this place."

Yes. Yes, I was. And I did, pardy in a rented beach cottage on St. Simons—both of us were under the spell of the place—and partly back in Chicago. (The story of all this is told in detail in an older book of mine, *St. Simons Memoir*, first published by Lippincott in 1978 and now available in the paperback edition issued in 1987 under the Jove imprint of Berkley.)

Of course, I intended to write only that one novel and then go on with our regular lives. Certainly, never having written a novel before, I had no notion then of ever being able to earn a living writing fiction. I had written fiction for years for Chi.cago and New York radio (remember radio dramas?), but no one, least of all I, could have foreseen what would happen as a result of *The Beloved Invader*, that first, quiet novel about Anson Greene Phelps Dodge, Jr., who rebuilt Christ Church in Frederica, St. Simons, in memory of his lovely bride, Ellen.

Oh, I had experienced a fair amount of publishing success but certainly not from my very first published book. That first little title was *Discoveries*. Zondervan Publishing House asked me to write it a few years after my conversion to Christianity and then slipped it onto the market so stealthily that I earned all of $94 during its entire first year of sales! Actually, most people believe *The Burden Is Light*, my second published book, to be my first.

I realize that my good fortune may be frustrating to most struggling authors because, after a story about me appeared in a magazine, still another publisher, Fleming H. Revell, asked me to write what turned out to be *The Burden Is Light*, the account of my life before and immediately after my conversion. *Burden* was another matter altogether. The publishers of *Discoveries* and the publishers of *The Burden*

Is Light were then in hot business competition. *Burden* benefited from this competition and, of course, so did I. There were national ads and there were huge, noisy, busy autographing parties not only in the vicinity of Chicago, where I then lived, but on both coasts.

In those noninflated days, the mid-1950s, I could have managed for nearly two years on my first Burden royalty check. I believe *Burden* earned something like $8,000! All the blame for this wide gap cannot be laid at the door of my first publisher. *Discoveries* was a quiet, unassuming, although evidently freshly worded, collection of essays about the discoveries I was making as I attempted to live my new life of faith. *Burden*, on the other hand, was an autobiographical story in which lots happened and with which readers have apparently been able to identify, because it's still in print (now also in a 1991 Doubleday edition) and for years has been called a classic, whatever that means.

After those first two titles, blind to the fact that I needed the help of an agent, I wrote inspirational book after book—each selling better than the one preceding—until that magical day after Thanksgiving 1961 when Joyce and I first drove over the causeway onto St. Simons Island at sundown. Even after the surprising sales of *The Beloved Invader* (which, remember, should be read third in the St. Simons Trilogy), I went on writing inspirational titles until my first and altogether memorable fiction editor, Tay Hohoff, at the J. B. Lippincott Company (now part of HarperCollins) convinced me that I had ample, rich material for a trilogy of novels. "One book in a trilogy feeds the others," she argued, and since I wanted very much to agree with her, of course, I signed for two more—*New Moon Rising* and *Lighthouse*.

Part of the way through the writing of *New Moon Ris-*

ing, Joyce and I had accepted the inevitable: as much as we loved our Chicago home, I, at least, no longer felt as I once had about Chicago. It's still a great place to visit, but long before I left, the city had changed so drastically from the place I loved in my university days spent there that I longed to leave. I had, in fact, been searching every part of this huge country as I flew, drove, and took trains north, south, east, and west to keep a hectic speaking schedule. I was looking for a place to live that would allow me the quiet and privacy needed to write books. We had found our place on St. Simons Island. We both knew it.

Joyce, who by then was also writing books, is far more people-oriented than I. I am not, by nature, a people person. My office, no matter where I live, is so full of people every day—novel characters more real to me much of the time than were they still alive and visible—that I can quickly feel crowded. I'm absolutely happy being alone. Solitude frees my thoughts.

Therefore, sometime in the summer of 1964, we bought four acres of palmetto-and-tree-choked land on the marshes of Glynn County, Georgia, in the vicinity of Anson Dodge's little white church and the churchyard where Joyce and I already owned our burial plots, bought even before we purchased the land where we meant to build our house. A writers' house, tall, steep-roofed, complementing the low, stretching landscape and as nearly as possible in the style of the old Island plantation houses, which by now we'd thoroughly researched.

Packing the contents of a three-storied townhouse and its basement was exhausting and emotional. We did love that old place and we had both lived most o f our adult lives in Chicago. Except for the years during World War II when

I worked out of New York, I had been a Chicagoan since the age of eighteen.

The years I spent in New York, where I knew no one, provided me with my first opportunity to get away from my overpeopled Chicago life to some semblance of solitude. But now, we were heading south forever. And miracle of miracles for a relatively unknown novelist (only *The Beloved Invader* had been published), Faith Brunson had agreed immediately when my publisher spoke to her about my doing an autographing party in the then revered, now vanished. Rich's downtown store in Atlanta.

Our plans were laid. I would keep one final scheduled speaking engagement at the Art Institute of Chicago and Joyce would drive my car to her parents' home in Indiana, after dropping me at the Chicago airport for my flight to Atlanta.

Reaching St. Simons to live at last in the much-used, drafty, but to us charming, little beach cottage called White Cap was almost reality. We'd leased the cottage, and our Chicago townhouse was sold (practically given away in order for us to get to St. Simons). But after Rich's and a visit for Joyce with her parents, there was still a three-week autographing tour before we could, for the first day and forever, call ourselves St. Simons Islanders.

We're Islanders now and have been for nearly three decades. Whether we know them personally or not, our neighbors are the more than fifteen thousand other persons who have succumbed to the charm of the Island's "dear dark woods," Sidney Lanier's description in his poem "The Marshes of Glynn." On May 4, 1991, when huge banners (even two enormous billboards) proclaimed EUGENIA PRICE DAY, the thirty busy years that followed our first settling into White Cap vanished from our minds; those enchanted early days came rushing back to us both, even though so much has changed. This small, sandy strip of tree-laden land between the Atlantic and the mainland has regrettably been overdeveloped, at least part of it. And yet, to us, some Island newness surprises every day; a recently hatched male painted bunting, still green like his mother and showing only a hint of the bright-blue head and red breast and chartreuse shawl he'll sport one day; the first red-purple French mulberry; the first tiny, white starflowers; the first clear-yellow gum leaf in late August; the quick, altogether tender way the Island renews itself after a bulldozer grinds through a patch of woods; the marsh greening in May where it touches our winding salt creeks . . . all these still hold us fast, refuse to let us go.

We are Islanders for always, because we wouldn't know how not to be.

PART II

EUGENIA PRICE

4

Finding Stories
and Titles

Since we found St. Simons Island, I have researched, written, and published eleven fairly long novels, all laid along the southeastern coast of the United States. There is fiction in each one, although most main characters are real persons who lived in the places and at the times I say they did. There is no way to write a novel without making use of the author's imagination. Love scenes and what someone thinks at night before falling asleep are simply not recorded in archives or courthouse records. If you've read my earlier book *St. Simons Memoir*, you know how I found the stories for the entire St. Simons Trilogy. You also know that each story has to begin inside my mind. I'm the one who has to live with those characters during the long months of writing.

Scarcely a week goes by that someone doesn't send a sheaf of family papers and a long letter insisting that I'm the only one who can turn "my grandparents' story into a fine novel." I'm grateful, of course, and I look each one over carefully, but not once has this worked for me. I can't explain why, but something has to happen in my brain, in my heart, to kick off the creative process. I don't understand the creative process. I just depend on it because I belong to the Creator. I believe any author, composer, or painter depends on God whether or not he or she knows it. Often, I get material about interesting persons who lived in another part of the country. But I am hopelessly hooked on the southeastern United States, and I doubt that at my age I'll ever bother to do all the research required in any place farther than a day's drive from my home.

Also, there is no way I can live long enough to begin to exhaust the story material around me. I have spent nearly thirty years doing research here and haven't scratched the surface of the lode of fully lived lives or their rich history. In my Georgia Trilogy I'm back again, using events right here on the Island and feeling as excited and eager to discover as ever. In fact, not only am I working in the same geographic region, but I'm covering the same period as in the Savannah Quartet— from the War of 1812 into the Civil War. The material, however, emphasizes a totally different perspective. No region was as homogeneous then as it is now.

Remember, oh, remember, especially if you are a writer yourself (or want to be, and some weeks it seems to me that almost everyone does), *that no author writes books for everyone.* Not everyone who reads is going to like the books of everyone who writes. Remembering this might make you a bit less critical of authors who shock or repulse you for whatever reason. You don't have to read their books. If my characters are "too good," no one has to read mine either.

I seriously doubt, no matter how smitten I was by my first awareness of the singular light in the thick woods of St. Simons Island, Georgia, that I would have thought of spend.ing the remainder of my life writing about the American South had I not already undergone a lasting conversion to Christianity. *God clarifies.*

A thoughtful gentleman wrote to me just last week asking, "How is it that a Yankee such as you could come down here and begin so quickly to understand Southerners? I know your books are read all over the English-speaking world, but we Southerners feel that you now belong to us. I admire the extraordinary talent of many of our native-born Southern writers, but I feel *you* somehow truly understand us and seem not to be trying to prove anything one way or another."

He's right. In a way I am an outsider to the American South. I've already written in articles and said in many lectures over the years that I held a prejudice a mile wide against all white Southerners when, in the 1960s, I first dis-covered Geor.gia and knew I wanted to move here. Have I lost that prejudice? Yes, but the day Joyce and I first crossed the South Carolina border, I felt as though I was entering a foreign land. Now I am as comfortable in the American South as I was in Ohio, where I began university life; and as I was in Illinois, where I continued with my studies and began to write for a living; and as I was in New York, where I lived and worked in radio during World War II. St. Simons Islanders, for the most part, allow me to be just me. They always have, especially back in the early days when, for almost a whole year, no one—not one single Islander—knew I'd ever published a book. Joyce and I wanted to keep it that way as long as possible. We let them think I was just beginning. I wanted the people I met to like me for myself I was drawn to the blessed anonymity I'd found on St. Simons—drawn to stay. I was at home in some special way that belonged to *me*.

No one could have grown up in a happier, more creative family than mine in my hometown of Charleston, West Virginia, but with the passing of the years. Charleston (where I haven't lived since I entered Ohio University at barely sixteen) came to be my parents' home. St. Simons is my home. All mine. My father was gone by the time I moved to St. Simons, but my wonderfully adaptive mother understood.

My home state of West Virginia was formed in the midst of the bitterness of the Civil War, and my history teachers had drummed pride into me that in order to remain in the Union, my state broke away from Virginia. I grew up thinking, when I thought about it at all, that I lived in a mid-Atlantic state, so when someone says that I understand Southerners because I grew up in a "Southern" state, I am still surprised. I know now, of course, that my state was a border state in the Civil War, but it did remain staunchly in the Union. This appealed to me. It still does. We are a *united* country. I am a citizen of the *United States* and proud of it.

"In *my* home state," I remember declaring to a college friend from Alabama, "we did not have rest rooms and drinking fountains marked Colored and White!" Of course, I didn't go to school with black children until I entered Ohio University, but since I wasn't yet sixteen at high school graduation, I hadn't bothered to think much about how incongruous that was. Although Mother and Dad saw to it that during my youth our black cook ate at the table with us, equality hadn't stirred my conscience until Rosa Parks took her seat in the front of that bus and Martin Luther King's brilliant, thoroughly Christian light flashed across our land. I grew angry then, and by the time Joyce and I headed my car onto the causeway that led to St. Simons, I was strongly supporting the civil rights movement.

Do I really understand Southerners? Yes, as much as I understand Ohioans, New Yorkers, and people from Nebraska, Florida, Texas, California, and Vermont. People can.not be stereotyped. Not by region or race or religion. Moving through my days as a follower of Jesus Christ has deepened my firm belief that He loves us all with equal intensity and equal loyalty. And with the writing of each new novel, my longing grows and grows to be able to make my nineteenth-century African-American characters as whole as I try to make my white characters. At first I was timid, almost afraid of trying. How could I know what it was like to be a black slave? Still, slaves in my chosen period of the nineteenth century were an integral, vital part of all Southern daily life. With all my heart and energy I try to avoid stereotypes—both of black slaves and of white slave masters.

Fortunately, I seem to have been accepted as simply another caring human being by my closest black friends. Some live on St. Simons, some in other parts of the country. The fine African-American novelist Tina McElroy Ansa is a constant, breathing part of my daily life. Tina helps me more than she guesses. To say that I believe in her as a writer is an understatement, but it is a glory to me that she also believes in me as a writer and as a friend. We've both long passed the place where we have any need to prove ourselves to each other. And when Tina thinks my black characters are well drawn, I rest in that. Just as I rest in the comments and letters from native white Southerners, many of whose ancestors were slave owners, who believe my white Southerners ring true.

Jo Couper Cauthorn, to whom I dedicated *Bright Captivity* and who, like Tina, is close and important to Joyce and to me, is a descendant of the Couper family featured in the Georgia Trilogy. Jo hates the "institution" as passionately as I do. "The old boy was a slaver," she said to me months before I finished *Bright Captivity*. "So, write John Couper that way. He hated the whole idea of being a slave owner, but he was." (That kind of liberty from a direct descendant truly frees an author!)

John Couper did dislike the institution of slavery. That is a fact. His letters prove it. Sapelo Island's Thomas Spalding, Couper's closest friend, also hated owning another human being. They both were slave owners, though. In fact, they broke Georgia law by importing the load of Ebos, whose story I used in the Prologue of *Bright Captivity*. Another valued African-American friend of mine is W. W. Law, founder of the wonderful black history museum in Savannah known as the King-Tisdell Cottage Foundation. "Don't forget. Miss Price," he said to me one day when the two of us were having lunch in the dining room of a Savannah hotel, "that regardless of what you may hear, both John Couper and Thomas Spalding were honorable gentlemen, both revered in their own time, both still revered today by older blacks."

You see, God has truly fair, open minds—cloaked in both black and white skin—scattered everywhere. I've simply been blessed to have found some of them.

Do I really understand Southerners? That's for you to

decide. I simply see them as people. I began to lose my prejudice against white Southerners as soon as I began to know them as warmhearted, gracious, intelligent people—some of them prickly in certain areas (but so am I), blind in other areas (but so am I). As soon as I began to know them as persons who, like you and me, weep beside open graves, laugh at themselves, love their country, lend helping hands to friends, I recognized them not only as Southerners but as people.

Novelists write about people. You who read my stuff seem never to tire of telling me that you just "don't forget my people." One dear, elderly lady from North Dakota wrote that "if I don't watch myself, I find I'm actually praying for your Mark Browning and I know perfectly well that you made him up!"

I had no trouble "making up" Mark Browning, a Yankee who fell, as did I, in love with the American South—with the city of Savannah. Mark Browning, like me, was simply a human being. Eliza Mackay, the favorite of almost everyone who reads my Savannah Quartet, was certainly a very human being. Miss Eliza was born in the South.

Did I understand her? I think I did, because I'd love to have had her as my friend. Southerners and Northerners are not that different one from the other—inside, where we all live. "We just can't get over how warm and friendly you girls are," our older, white St. Simons friends used to tell Joyce and me. "We thought Yankees were short-spoken and curt—downright cold. You're not a bit that way!" They had come to know us as people.

As with my conversion to Christianity, my conversion to the South found me, in a way, with "all things made new." I stepped back, as it were (probably not realizing that I was doing it), and took a fresh look at all of us in the North and in the South. I chose this place, but I don't necessarily consider myself a white Southerner. I am just a person, convinced that when the chips are down, when grief or happiness overwhelms us, we feel the same agony or joy whether we happen to live in Mobile, Alabama, or in Bangor, Maine.

At the conclusion of the third book in my St. Simons Trilogy, I was faced for the first time with finding an entirely new story—or thought I was. *Lighthouse, New Moon Rising*, and *The Beloved Invader* had all been written, their promotion tours were at an end. By then I knew several prominent Southern historians, among them my already much-admired friend the late Walter Charlton Hartridge, of Savannah, to whom I'd dedicated *Lighthouse*. Walter had shown me a caliber of historical research and stored knowledge I hadn't known existed until I met him and his lovely wife, Susan. It had been Walter who confirmed my guess that the main character in *Lighthouse*, James Gould, probably did obtain his St. Marys timber tract from an eccentric, charming, impractical Georgian named John McQueen, then living in luxury and style in Spanish East Florida because had he tried to stay in Georgia, he would have been in debtors' prison. Walter Hartridge was known in the world of southeastern history for his work on the man the Spanish renamed Don Juan McQueen, and he had edited a superb book of Don Juan's letters to his family, which I owned.

If you've read *Lighthouse*, you know that Don Juan, in his custom-made, gold-lace-trimmed uniform, was a minor character. You also know that he was indeed a "character"— uniquely so. I loved Don Juan, so I drew him from fact, but I imbued him with the wonderfully lovable idiosyncrasies of both Walter Hartridge and my own adored father.

But I swear to you that until my then fiction editor, the late Tay Hohoff, came to spend a few days with me at the conclusion of our work on the St. Simons Trilogy, I hadn't thought once of doing an entire novel about Don Juan McQueen! It would take too much space to go into adequate detail about what Tay Hohoff was really like. Could I just say that she was one of the best editors in New York publishing, several years older than I, brilliant, eccentric, and, to me, as genuine in friendship as she was in her profession. Tay seemed not to need sleep or food. Just a good stiff drink and books and Mozart. The second night she was here on St. Simons, staying in our guest wing, she and I were still downstairs at 3 A.M. talking in the living room about a new contract she was offering me and what might be the subject of my next novel. I was so tired I hadn't had a clear thought in hours, but I loved Tay so much and cherished every moment of her company to such an extent that I was not going to let her know, if I could help it, how bushed I really was.

Our talk veered back to the St. Simons Trilogy, and for a reason I was far too foggy to understand, Tay suddenly began to talk about the dinner scene in *Lighthouse* at Major Pierce Butler's Hampton Plantation, in which James Gould, John Couper, and Don Juan McQueen had hit upon the idea that McQueen might be able to help James Gould locate property on the St. Marys River on the Georgia-Florida border. What, I wondered, did that scene have to do with the direction of this crazy, middle-of-the-night conversation?

I vow it was totally by chance, but *by chance* I just happened to mention that I could never think of McQueen merely as Savannah gentleman *John* McQueen. Because he was such an adventurer, such a gambler with his own funds and properties, so colorful, such a perpetual optimist, to me he would always be *Don Juan McQueen*.

The Georgia Power Company might as well have shot an extra bolt of electricity through my living room when I spoke those words. Tay jumped to her feet, held out her arms to me—she was not the demonstrative type—and snapped: "Well! I thought you'd *never* bring up his name. Do you realize I literally had to pry it out of you?"

In her fertile editor's brain, she had made the trip south with the express idea of sounding me out on doing my next novel about Don Juan, The woman was Just too stubborn, too wise, too aware, that unless the author brought it up, the idea was probably not going to work. Never mind that she forced it out of me when I was too weary to realize, until I was upstairs and in my own bed, what she had done.

All she said after hugging me was, "Now get to bed. You've been asleep for two hours anyway. I just had to hear you mention his name yourself We'll talk about the book tomorrow." I was wide awake by then because the whole episode had begun to strike me as funny and as eccentric as both Don Juan and Tay really were.

It had, of course, been Tay who started me thinking in terms of writing in series. She had died by the time I tackled a quartet, but the series pattern is set and I'm too old now to change. I wrote *Don Juan McQueen* (neither of us once considered the use of a title other than his wonderful name), and in doing extensive research for the book, with and without Walter Hartridge, at the St. Augustine Historical Society, I became absolutely enamored of northern Florida history. So, for the next novel in what turned out to be the Florida Trilogy, my dear friend Eugenia Arana, then chief researcher at the historical society on St. Augustine's Charlotte Street, "found" *Maria* with me. Because she was Puerto Rican, Eugenia could read all those invaluable, informative Spanish documents in the archives, and together we fell in love with the Charlestonian Mary Evans. Beautiful, feminist Mary Evans, under the magic of the old Spanish-British city of St. Augustine, became *Maria*, the town's prosperous, influential, professional woman—a highly sought-after midwife. She also became the main character in my second Florida novel, *Maria*. Because *Inside One Authors Heart* is being written especially for my readers, it may be well to say right here that what turned out to be the Florida Trilogy is a trilogy only geographically. The three tales in *Don Juan McQueen*, *Maria*, and *Margaret's Story* are not necessarily related to each other.

Even though Walter Hartridge died suddenly, just as I was planning a *Maria* research trip to Charleston with him and Susan, I do have the solace of knowing that in his highly perceptive way, Walter approved of my doing Maria's story. In fact, the last letter I received from him (and still cherish) informed me that "Maria Evans is just right for you. Go ahead!"

Once *Maria* was written and published and I'd recovered somewhat from the exhausting autographing tour in its behalf, I began to wonder which story I'd do next. In no way was I willing to relinquish northern Florida history, which to this day I find fascinating. But I had covered the earlier period in which Spanish East Florida became British East Florida and then, within a few years, Spanish again, so I thought in terms of a slightly later time period. Also, through Walter Hartridge I had come to know and to depend on Jacksonville's historian nonpareil, Dena Snodgrass, who in her genteel way is altogether colorful and stimulating and attractive and *knows* Florida history.

Through my previous work in northern Florida history and because she had written one or two excellent pieces about me for her newspaper, Jacksonville's *Florida Times-Union*, another friend (who would become still more special with the passing of the years), Ann Hyman, entered my life. Ann's own writing talent is one of my favorite subjects these days, not only for her work for her newspaper but for her superb, one-of-a-kind memoir. *Chaos Clear as Glass* (Marietta, Ga.; Long- street Press, 1991).

Joyce loves to tell stories about the amazing instances of serendipity I keep experiencing in the writing of almost all these novels, and Ann Hyman and Dena Snodgrass were the unwitting central characters in one of the most intriguing episodes. While I was hunting a story to complete the Florida Trilogy, Ann wrote and published an excellent article on a quaint Episcopal chapel at Hibernia, Florida, near Green Cove Springs. Because I try never to miss anything Ann writes, I had read her article about Margaret Fleming and her chapel in the woods right after Dena had suggested Margaret as a subject for my next novel. Here is the odd part. As always, I admired Ann's article; I also thought Dena's material on Margaret Fleming had definite merit, but for a reason I can't now explain, I turned down the story. Too many years have passed for me to remember exactly what turned me around, but both Joyce and I believe that it must have been my first actual look at that dear little weathered chapel and its cemetery nestled under giant magnolias at Hibernia.

Whatever it was, I was off again— gone from this century as only those who are with me day in and day out understand. I was living in Margaret's time, leaning fully on Dena's expertise and willingness to take on the huge research project with me. Dena and Hester Williams, Margaret's descendant, were my stays. I don't remember more than the usual turmoil in untangling events and dates and my normal resistance to nineteenth-century people who had too many children, but I do remember that I worried more than usual about the title. Along with the writing of the novel, also carried another manuscript—published simultaneously—titled *Diary of a Novel*. Writing two books at once is pretty crazy, of course, but because of Dena and Hester and my good friends at the St. Augustine Historical Society, especially Jackie Fretwell, I enjoyed the work even though I endured a severe case of vertigo for the entire time. Enjoyed it all, that is, except for the nagging worry about a title. Titles are often a headache to ail author. Only *Don Juan McQueen, Maria, Lighthouse*, and *Before the Darkness Falls* seemed settled from the start.

Early in the writing of the story about Margaret Fleming, our longtime friend Elsie Goodwillie grew too ill to continue helping me with my mail and retyping my scratched-up drafts of manuscript. I don't remember any fanfare, but there should have been one when, through a mutual friend, Emmy Minor, Eileen Humphlett, my talented, caring assistant, entered my life. Without her beside me, I simply would not be functioning these days as I still am. Anyone who knows me at all knows that. And Eileen can tell you how I— all of us—fidgeted and fretted over Margaret's title. I wrote the book, rewrote it, and turned it over to her to type; she was at least half finished when one day on the telephone, in her typically contained way, with just an edge of excitement showing in her voice, Eileen asked, "Why not call the book what we've been calling it all along— *Margaret's Story*?" Of

I've always disliked dolls!

With Joyce in our backyard.

(Courtesy of the Atlanta Journal Constitution.)

Signing books on the trunk of someone's car with Ed Waters.

Me, Sarah Bell Edmond, and Miss Daisy (Joyce) in our kitchen.

Oxford Bookstore in Atlanta with my publicist, Kellen Archer.

Billboard on causeway to
St. Simons.

The important front row
at band stand.
Left to right: Kay
CJarland, Sarah
Plemmons, Ana Bel
Lee Washington, Tina
McElroy Ansa, Nancy
Goshorn, Lila Karpf, Bebe
Cole, Carolyn Blakemore,
Jane Schorn, Ellen Archer,
and Mildred Huie.

Eileen Humphlett leading
me after morning session
on Eugenia Price Day.

Patient readers
waiting outside
St. Simon's Club
for my scribble.

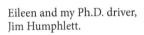

Eileen and my Ph.D. driver,
Jim Humphlett.

With dinner master of ceremonies,
wonderful Fred Bentley.

Nancy Goshorn, me, and Glenn Smith at *Stranger in Savannah* party at St. Marys, Georgia.

Me, looking old and tired but happy, and Steve Rubin at Old Plantation Club dinner (end of EP Day).

Joyce and Jo Couper Cauthorn at dinner speakers' table.

At dinner: me, dear friend Dot Martin (*standing*), Steve, and Joyce.

At dinner: me with (*left to right, seated*) Carolyn, Lila, and beloved, hilarious Juanelle Edwards.

Dear Elizabeth Harris moving our hearts toward singing "Amazing Grace."

Tina McElroy Ansa and Joyce, collapsed, at end of autographing at St. Simons Island Club.

After autographing party in Savannah: Esther Shaver, Ed Waters, me, Ruth Waters, Eileen, Nancy, and Ed Shaver.

Holding Jim Gould's
little tin lantern
(*Lighthouse*).

With my brother,
Joe.

course, it was the perfect title in all ways. And we *had* all been calling it that, almost from the beginning.

Soon after Tay Hohoff died in the 1970s, I finished a two-book contract with Harper & Row (now HarperCollins). Because Tay had said, right up to the end, that Carolyn Blakemore was the right editor for me, I moved to Doubleday. Carolyn, as was becoming common in New York publishing (and now seems almost a fad) had left Lippincott to work as a senior editor at Doubleday. Frequently in such shifts, authors tend to fall between the cracks, even authors who appear to be valuable to publishers. For my next novel I was therefore starting over with a new publishing house, where almost no one but Car.olyn Blakemore knew me and where, again. I'd have to do a lot of exhausting promotion in order to prove myself.

When, at the simultaneous publication of *Margaret's Story* and *Diary of a Novel*, I had fulfilled my Harper contracts, Carolyn, whom Joyce and I had known and loved for years, flew to St. Simons to talk about my first book for Doubleday. (It had been Carolyn who called me the morning our beloved Tay Hohoff had been found dead in her apartment.)

To this day, in the late afternoon as Joyce and I sit reading in our living room, I think often of the way Carolyn looked sitting beside me in the tall Queen Anne chair where she always sits when visiting us. "We'd like you to do a huge novel on Atlanta," she said. "We" meant Doubleday, of course, and I listened alertly.

But then I asked, "Hasn't another writer, named Margaret Mitchell, already done a story about Atlanta?" When Carolyn laughed (we've always done a lot of that), I jumped back in: "I'd love to do a book on Savannah, though."

Carolyn agreed at once, made the best offer I'd had to date, and so began the Savannah Quartet. Of course, we talked during that visit of only one novel, but I hadn't worked on it for more than a few weeks when I realized that the old series pattern was indelibly part of my creative process. You guessed it. We contracted for a second book. The first novel Carolyn and I did together was, of course, easily titled *Savannah*. The second novel in the Savannah Quartet had no title until Joyce and I had fled to an obscure, tiny South Carolina town to escape the mail and the telephone and to give me time to read what I'd written. Out of the blue, one afternoon in our modest motel room, while Joyce was grocery shopping, the title came to me: *To See Your Face Again*.

Not long after, when I was in Atlanta promoting a small book called At Home on St. Simons for my friends at Peachtree Publishers, Faith Brunson strongly urged me to stop trying to handle my ever-increasing publishing affairs alone and talk to her longtime friend Lila Karpf, who would be, she declared, "the perfect agent" for me. I did and she was and she still is.

In retrospect it now seems no time at all passed, after Joyce agreed with me that *To See Your Face Again* was the right title, before Lila called from New York to spring the great news that she had just reached an agreement with Doubleday for still two more novels in what would be the Savannah Quartet—an agreement far more rewarding than this author, at least, had ever imagined.

Because she knew I had written only nonfiction books before she and I began work on the St. Simons Trilogy, Tay had urged me to stick with true stories based on the lives of real people. By then I was also eager to do that, because you, my readers, seemed to love knowing that the characters actually lived, and you were reveling in the adventure of looking up their house sites and tombstones in both Florida and Georgia.

Of course, the more of my books readers buy, the more royalties I earn, but this author makes no bones about wanting—deep down inside—to please her readers for far more reasons than the obvious need to make a living. Some may not beheve that. The core of my loyal readers will. We trust each other. I have no intention now o f ever departing from real stories about real people, even though pure fiction is far more fun and much easier. When I do fictionalize any of my main characters, as I most certainly did in the Savannah Quartet, I do my best to make it plain in my Afterword that I've done so. The entire Browning family came out of my head with the prodding of a few old letters I once found. I made up Mark Browning's name and the names o f his family members, but I wove their lives, with as much historical plausibility as possible, into the actual records of the Mackays and the Stileses.

Finding titles for *Before the Darkness Falls* and *Stranger in Savannah* illustrates the vastly different ways in which authors or editors come up with exactly what to call a book. I had the right title for *Before the Darkness Falls* the same day the idea for the theme came to mind, but believe me, this is a rarity. I knew from research that Robert E. Lee would be in the final scene and what close friends he and Eliza Mackay were. The title came from one of the lines she spoke to Mark Browning the night Lee was a dinner guest at the Mackay house: "...such a darkness could fall over this land..." On the other hand, the title for *Stranger in Savannah* was a gradual finding. I was probably three-quarters of the way through the first draft when I realized that there were at least three "strangers in Savannah" at that time: Indian Mary, Mark, and General William Sherman himself These two titles, along with *The Beloved Invader*—which just appeared as I waited in a doctor's office for my first pair of reading glasses—have been among the most successful of my titles.

Now I am embarked on yet another trilogy of novels beginning once more on St. Simons Island. This is called the Georgia Trilogy because the third book shifts locale from St. Simons to Marietta, Georgia, near Atlanta. Where did I get the skeleton of the story of Anne Couper Fraser? From the same beautiful source to whom I've been turning since my first attempt at fiction in *The Beloved Invader*. I hied myself to visit my time-proven, cherished friend, historian Burnette Vans-tory, who still lived in her home on East Beach here on St. Simons. Burney Vanstory, as thousands of readers know, is the widely read author of *Georgia's Land of the Golden Isles* (Athens; University of Georgia Press, 1956, 1970), without which I'd have been hopelessly lost over the past years as a novelist. Not only is Burney my close friend, she is a skillfully accurate historian and blessedly readable. I'm sure copies of her Georgia's Land of the Golden Isles are on thousands and thousands of bookshelves all over the United States and Can.ada, because for thirty-five years it has remained one of the bestselling books for natives and tourists in love with the Golden Isles of Georgia.

After the final book in the Savannah Quartet was published and my last autographing tour was finished, I knew I must discuss with Burney two or three ideas I'd gleaned through the years from my own research on St. Simons and from having used her book as a novelist's bible. If anyone could guide me on which of the St. Simons families to settle on as the main characters in the new Georgia Trilogy, it would be Burney. She knew, because she knows me so well, that through the long years since the publication of the first Island trilogy, readers had never stopped asking that I do more novels set on St. Simons. Burney now lives in her own attractive apartment in the Roswell, Georgia, home of her granddaughter and namesake, Burnette Sheffield, but I do my best to keep her posted on the progress of my work on the story of Anne Couper Fraser, daughter of a colorful Scot, John Couper of Cannon's Point. The day I visited Burney to discuss the ideas I'd mulled over was the day *Bright Captivity* began. As usual, I didn't have a title yet, but it must have been close to the surface of my consciousness. Anne had in all ways been captured by British Lieutenant John Fraser, and through good times and bad the captivity remained, for Anne, bright.

For me, too.

Before I leave the subject of titles, I might give you a smile by telling you that while everyone in the publishing world believes titles are all-important, some downright humorous distortions can take place no matter how hard we try to make sure a title is both colorful and easy to remember. My first moment of amusement came with my first novel. *The Beloved Invader*, which we thought a good title. But within weeks after its publication, someone wrote to tell me how much she'd loved *The Beloved Intruder*. Funnier yet (keep in mind that the main character, Anson Dodge, was a Christian priest), still another reader declared he'd found *The Beloved Infidel* intensely interesting.

New Moon Rising once became *New Moon over My Shoulder*, and just last month came a card from my friends

Esther and Maryann, at Shaver's Fine Books in Savannah, which read, "Add these to your list: *Bright Activity* and *Bright Capacity.*" I've also been told that someone called Doubleday to ask the publication date of the sequel to *Bright Charity.*

It could just be that we who labor over the making of titles take it all a bit too seriously.

EUGENIA PRICE

5

How Do I
Do Research?

A complete answer to the question of how I do research, which I'm asked almost as often as any other, would itself fill a book. Much of what I've already written in these pages concerns my research as well as that others have done for me and with me during the past years. Each research project is different because each book brings its own particular needs, and although I find it far less forbidding than in the early years, research is still the fundamental preparation.

There is nothing to stop a writer of fiction from fictionaliz.ing anything. Still, I find that I care deeply that the factual material I use is as accurate as I can possibly manage. Especially now that I know certain history teachers are using my novels as a means of grabbing the attention of their students, of interesting them in learning what took place in past centuries that may have molded the United States into whatever condition it now finds itself.

I don't honestly remember details of how I did my research before and during the writing of some earlier novels. There.fore, as an illustration, I'll share here what's fresh in my mind from work during the background digging for *Bright Captivity.* I have never been more drawn to a character than I was to Anne Couper, daughter of John Couper of Cannon's Point, perhaps because Couper himself has long been a favorite. There is certainly no dearth of material available about him. I had to be careful while writing *Bright Captivity* not to allow John Couper to take over the story. Because I like him so much and so many of his actual letters are still extant, and so much has been written about him, the old boy would have kept striding into scene after scene if I hadn't controlled him.

Descendants of the Couper family gave our local Coastal Georgia Historical Society a valuable collection of Couper letters, and from them and from other family letters found in Savannah archives, I learned about his wife, Rebecca, and their deep devotion to each other; about John Couper's delicious humor, his admiration of and amusementat his first son, James Hamilton Couper, whom he called the Old Gentleman. I also learned that Anne, his firstborn daughter, was the apple of Couper's eye.

As to Anne's genuine romance with her British Lieuten.ant John Fraser, I found ample confirmation in family letters. I read and reread Anne's very first letter written to John right after he captured her on Cumberland Island near the end of the War of 1812. That letter left no doubt in my mind that Anne Couper did fall instantly in love.

My close friend of many years, Nancy Goshorn, knows a lot more about John Couper and his daughter, Anne, than

I do, since it is she who is now my expert conduit between the copious archival records of all the persons in my novels and me. Many experts helped invaluably with the always complex research in my earlier days, when Joyce and I bumbled about alone, and my thanks still flow to them. But now, at long last, I can afford to have a fulltime researcher, and in Nancy I have one of the best. Unlike me, she has the infinite patience to wade through page after page of hard-to-read, faded script in the old letters kept (thank heaven) by members of the Couper family. She read and read and read in the local archives here at our St. Simons Museum of Coastal History, at the Brunswick Regional Library, at the St. Simons Library, and at Brunswick College. She then stayed in Savannah for long periods of time reading the excellent collections of Couper letters housed in the Georgia Historical Society, where she was skillfully helped by Director Anne Smith and by Tracy Bearden and Jan Flores. Always, she found Linda King, director of our local historical society, and her staff eager to help us. The same was true of Virginia Boyd, Al Spivey, Marcia Hodges, and Doro-thy Houseal in the college and public libraries in Brunswick, Georgia.

Both Nancy and I wonder if we'd ever make it through another novel without the professional expertise of these research librarians. Research for one of these long novels in the very area where its characters once lived has consequently become more a group project than a lonely writing job. It helps me more than anyone guesses to know not only that there is a community of other people around me who care about what I'm doing, but that you out there who read are also pulling for me to turn it all into a story.

One of the most valuable resources to any writer of historical novels is the huge number of published books.

When I realized that *Bright Captivity* would require details about London and Scotland in the early nineteenth century, I thought about going abroad myselfor sendingJoyce or Eileen or Nancy, butI knew the settings would be vastly changed by now. It so happened that Frances Daugherty, another extremely helpful and encouraging descendant of Anne and her husband, John Fraser, wrote that she was going to London right when I needed someone to go. Frances found, and took pictures of, the very house where the couple had lived as newlyweds with John's father, James Fraser. Then, along with a couple of old books Joyce and her parents had brought back from a long-ago trip to England and Scotland, Nancy found some wonder.ful books via the inter-library loan system, all of which she immediately began to digest. Her patience and love of detail (keep in mind my lack of both) serve my purposes exactly. She reads and sifts facts and inserts carefully notated slips of paper, so that when it's time for me to learn enough of what she's found in order to write about it, the information is all set. For me, hours and hours of research time have been saved. My estimate is that because I now have Nancy to do this for me, you have each new novel in your hands at least six months earlier than you might otherwise have it. (And many of you do, thank heaven, go on fussing at me for being so slow!) Just in passing, we had learned from Couper descendants that Anne and John Fraser knew Sir Walter Scott in the days before he was knighted and that they even owned an autographed novel of his. Nancy did one of her more impressive digests when she summarized a two-volume biography of Scott; therefore I had no trouble capturing the man's personality and thinking for *Bright Captivity*.

Another gracious area historian saved me from mistakes by sharing her detailed knowledge of the history of Cumberland Island, the second island south of St. Simons, in the days of the second war with Great Britain, later called the War of 1812. Her name is Eloise Bailey, of St. Marys, Georgia, and not only was she able to refer us to authentic records and books on the subject, she stayed beside us ready to answer our many questions. We are forever grateful, too, to Peggy Buchan, another fine St. Simons artist; her husband, Danny; and the Sea Island Company for inestimable help and ready access to the ruins of Cannon's Point and Lawrence, the plantations where the Coupers and the Frasers lived.

Research is quite like a treasure hunt. One contact leads to another, and often a closed door—finding nothing—is as valuable as the always exciting discovery of an actual document. The director of old Fort Jackson in Savannah, Scott Smith, has helped me for many years. He is a top authority on the old military. Since it's always hard for me to understand anything military, that I found Scott so agreeable and so much fun helped endlessly. He was blunt, though, about knowing little of British naval uniforms worn in the War of 1812, so he referred me to Joe Thompson, superintendent of Wormsloe Plantation Historic Site. Off Nancc and I went to spend a day with him. Joe knew, and even had a picture of, the very uniform Anne's Lieutenant John Fraser would have worn.

Before the publication of *Bright Captivity*, I started the second novel in the Georgia Trilogy— as I always try to do before the inevitable interruption of having a new book in the stores. Will I, once I finish this little book, be able to pick right up on the sequel to *Bright Captivity*? In a way, yes, but I'm not as far along as I had thought. Further research, in the interim, has thrown up at least a small roadblock. Nancy has just spent another week in Savannah poring over microfilm of the *Darien Gazette* from the years 1818-1828. In my previously written manuscript pages, I had begun the novel in 1820, because no one was able to find the precise date on which Anne and John Fraser returned to Georgia from London. In those early pages I fictionalized the arrival of Anne, John, and their daughter at the Savannah waterfront. In that version I selected a friend of John Couper's to meet them. What did Nance discover in those old *Darien Gazettes*? Only that the poor friend's wife had been killed in a buggy accident a day or so before I had the Frasers arriving! That scene won't work. Now what will I do?

One of the most serendipitous happenings I've ever experienced in all the research I've done—and there have been many—came about through one o f my closest friends, Bobby Bennett, for years my right hand in research at the Georgia Historical Society in Savannah. Bobby, now living in New York, had access to the libraries of Columbia University, where she found an old travel guide—a copy o f which John and Anne Fraser might well have used during their early days as bride and groom when John was showing London to Anne. The guide was published, as I recall, in the year 1815, the year before the newlyweds reached London. Of course, I made extensive use of it so that I could be certain, when I took them down a particular street in a rented carriage, the street existed when they were in London.

There is no adequate means to explain the complexities of research. Success in finding only what is actually needed is the trick and often keeps several persons busy. I have always tried to pay adequately for research help, although some who are on the staffs of our fine southeastern archives refuse payment. In those instances I do my best to compensate with contributions to the societies that employ them. I have found that only the kindest, most skillful people work among these old records. They're a special breed, because I know what most of them earn. We do become friends, and I can tell you firsthand that they all work for love of history and the fulfillment they receive from helping otherwise unknowing people like me.

If you have learned something new from my novels—if you love history and like the novels, at least in part, because of the history in them—tip your hats to those who give and give to me as I write, and by all means, please contribute to historical archives somewhere! Their funding is always in short supply, especially these days when all libraries are so strapped for funds. On TV the other evening I heard one librarian say something I wish I'd said: "Wouldn't it be wonderful if our government changed priorities, so that libraries got complete funding and the Pentagon had to give bake sales in order to make it?"

One thing I can tell you emphatically is that without libraries of all kinds, you would not have had even one of my novels to read. No one would have been able to say to me, as so many of you do say, "I never knew history could be so stimulating. Thank you for all the worthwhile, interesting hours you've given me."

The key to doing research for all these novels is a detailed chronology. In the early days I usually compiled my own. In fact, for some books I had composed so many different chronologies I was forced to condense them into a single one I could keep beside me, checking off as I covered certain dates and events. Nance has a brand new chronology waiting for my use in the two remaining novels in the

Georgia Trilogy as soon as *Inside One Author's Heart* is on its way to my publishers in New York.

How does one make a chronology? By reading, studying, taking notes, jotting down events gleaned both from family trees and from reference books, and by spending hours and hours to compare and notate pertinent facts from old letters. Happenings in the United States and in the world must be tracked at the same time. One must also guard against including too many events not directly related to the main story, against diminishing the characters by distracting the reader with an overload of history. Research can't be fully explained, but aside from accuracy, nothing is more important than selectivity. Nancy Goshorn is a research *natural*, but once the digging is done, I must then learn all the facts so well that when you read, you believe that you and I are both there—living our lives at that time in that place.

Research becomes much like light itself. It reveals struggles, scandals, poor judgments, that might otherwise stay hid.den in the dark. History can show how many wars could have been averted. I believe that if cooler heads had prevailed in the years before our Civil War, negotiations would eventually have worked. Of course, if we don't learn from history, knowing facts helps very little. But *if we choose to learn*, enlightenment comes.

I once read that Cicero said: "To be ignorant of what happened before you were born is to be forever a child." He was right.

6

My St. Simons
Support Group

Four absolutely necessary people make my writing life possible. They are, individually and together, the reason that at age 75 I plan to keep on writing books at the same old tempo. The truth is that because of these four—Joyce Blackburn, Eileen Humphlett, Nancy Goshorn, and Sarah Bell Edmond—I've never been happier.

It was my agent, Lila Karpf, who named them Genie's St. Simons Support Group, and in a way Lila herself is an integral part of the Group, although she lives and works in New York. The average agent doesn't call a client every day, but Lila rarely misses a day. Especially since she flew down for my big celebration in May, she delights us all by feeling a part of us now. Each time she calls with news of any kind, I then report to the St. Simons Support Group.

Joyce must come first, because unless she's out grocery shopping (she vows I'm not good at it) or with friends, she is with me more than is any other person on earth. Our house was designed so that each of us has plenty of privacy—we don't get in each other's hair—but we do live together and share the same joys and sorrows, the same food, most of the same irritations, the same knocked-out humor, the same TV shows, and often the same books and magazines.

We've never bothered, in all the more than thirty years we've lived together, to divide up household chores. Now, with my days steadily concentrated on writing, my obligations increased in all directions, she simply goes about taking on my household responsibilities as though we'd come to a decision about it. We didn't. In a relationship as close and as compatible as ours, there is little need for decisions.

She also does most o f the driving. She enjoys "going down the road." Not me. I love being *inside* working on a novel—at my desk, looking at the beauty *outside* without the nuisance of being hot or slapping at deerflies and gnats, both of which we have in abundance on St. Simons. If I need a research session with Nance, I hop in my own car and drive down to her house. If I need a haircut, I drive to Rosemary's shop. Usually, though, I find myself blithely climbing in the passenger seat, expecting Joyce to take me wherever we're going. Because I lose track of time when I'm writing hard, Joyce has casually begun to bring our lunch upstairs so that we can watch the CNN noon news, thereby giving Sarah Bell liberty to shine up our kitchen and living room without us underfoot.

In a way, we take turns fixing dinner, although Joyce invariably has the best menu ideas. My specialties (I have only four) are sauteed chicken livers with rice; hot, *hot* Mexican chili; spaghetti sauce and vermicelli, which I dare anyone to top; and scrambled eggs. Because Joyce knows my limitations in the kitchen, she keeps our favorite frozen dinners in the freezer for those evenings when we're both too weary or dull to think up a meal from scratch. I must add here (mainly because I want her to read it when she goes over this manuscript line by line as she's done with every book of mine since we began our lives together) that I am—no matter how preoccupied or how lost in the nineteenth century—always aware that most of what goes on around our blessed house in the woods at Frederica is geared to what I am doing at the moment. Joyce's grace in adapting herself to me is flexible and lasting. I do everything my often cluttered mind permits to make her life good, but I know that without ever making me feel guilty, she does conduct her own life around my oddball needs and schedule. And she does it with humor, at least most of the time.

Fortunately for us both, she is far more of a people person than I, so she writes more notes, makes more local and long-distance calls to those in need of contact, and even finds time for visiting. I hope our friends know that when they hear from Joyce, I'm in on it too. I want her to know that I'm also aware of the wistfulness in her voice when she refers (always lightly) to the "old days" when there was plenty of time to listen to music, to watch birds together, to search out hidden, tree-lined roads in the coastal beauty spots on and around St. Simons. Sometimes I wish I weren't so busy, because my busyness is the reason we seldom have time for idling unless we're away from the Island—me without this typewriter.

Joyce Blackburn and I have lived our lives together, both as writers and best friends, for more than thirty years, day in and day out, but not for one minute have I ever, ever tired of her company. I can pay her no higher compliment, since my greatest spiritual lack (and I think it is a spiritual lack) has always been my tendency to quickly become bored. Our politics are alike, and our ways of seeing God are so similar we stay amazed, because He became real to us both in widely differing ways. Our tastes in music, drama, books, style, and architecture are startlingly similar, but we are far from identical. She loves ballet! I can take it or leave it. She is far fonder of the legitimate theater than I am, but we both loathe rock and roll, although we've tried to open ourselves to it. I'm sure we could be called dated traditionalists, since we'll take Billie Holiday anytime over any woman singer today, except perhaps Cleo Laine. Both of us love our country too much, I think. Even steeped in history and current news, we go on expecting too much from our so-called leadership. We are both strong environmentalists—Joyce a more active one than I, not only because she stays better informed but because she doesn't seem to mind all the bags standing around full of old newspapers and cans and bottles for recycling. I sometimes object and become annoyed. She doesn't. We therefore recycle everything.

Do we have fun? You bet. Between us we know hundreds of people. Neither of us knows any who laugh more, share more, have more fun together, than the two of us. We both dislike games with rules—except baseball. Neither of us could sit still for a game of cards, but the Atlanta Braves can make the evenings fly by—when they're winning. Because I stay put at my desk most of the time and Joyce flies about, I am always losing track of her in our big, two-storied house. I call, "Where are you?"

She invariably answers, "Here!" But where is here? Of course, if she began to answer, "I'm in my office" or even "downstairs," it would help, but it would also spoil the game.

If you've read even one Afterword I always add to every novel I write (many of you vow you read it first), you already know that my dependence on Joyce's editing skills is almost childlike. I can be writing along in one of those occasional streaks when the story flows easily, when things seem to be working, and never have to stop because I know that Joyce will "fix it." This she does for love's sake. I do it for her when she's writing, but I'm not as good at it as she is because it takes patience and time. No matter how long I live, I'll undoubtedly go right on hurrying, driving myself, and loving every minute of it. Our tempos may be the major source of difference. Joyce seldom seems hurried. I seldom take it easy. Unless I'm concentrating, I'm fidgety. Of course, I know she's a marvelous actress. She earned her living by acting in the old days in Chicago radio, so maybe she fools me.

People coming to our house for the first time usually comment on the "peace in the place." Our harmony is God's doing. We are not geared alike and yet we're compatible and creative together.

Joyce will, of course, have gone over every word in this book. She has already slipped onto my desk three note pages of things I need to remember to write about. I have used most of them. No wonder we get along. Not only do I trust her heart, her every intention toward me, I trust her fine mind and her superior taste.

She also trusts mine.

Eileen Humphlett, known as our Overqualified Keeper, can, I think, sometimes read Joyce more accurately than I do. Aside from Eileen's regular morning call to me, she and Joyce talk more often. After all. I'm usually in the nineteenth century! I also have a hard-and-fast rule that I do not break up a workday. Errands or other business, take Joyce and Eileen out often and they frequently "do lunch." Their close relationship is one of my pure joys. What if they didn't like each other? Where would I be? Caught in the middle. Joyce and I are extremely fond of all three of Eileen's children—Carrie Beth, Mark, and Jay. They are certainly rewards to both their parents—to Eileen and to her handsome, fun husband, Jimmy—but they are also awards to them. All three are already successful, attractive human beings and still in their twenties. They would rather come home when there is free time from college or work than go anywhere else. Eileen knows I'm proud of her offspring, but it's Joyce, of course, who keeps up with their birthdays (with everyone's birthday!), and it's Joyce who always knows and remembers when one of the young Humphletts is due home for a visit.

One of Eileen's favorite T-shirts—given to her by Joyce—bears the lettering MY REAL NAME IS NOT MOM. That gives you a good idea of Eileen's brand of crisp humor, because although my experience with motherhood is limited to novels, I can't imagine any woman's being a more successful mom. Still she never, never neglects me, and during the more than twelve years we've been together, not once has she ever made me feel that my requests intrude. That may not seem very remarkable, but it really is, because although her work schedule is mostly under her control, at certain times my professional need of her becomes almost total. I try never to interfere with her weekends with Jimmy, but I don't remember many weekends when she hasn't called at least once just to ask, "What's going on up there? Is everyone all right?"

She knows (now that I understand what it means to

her) that she is free to play tennis anytime, and although I don't remember to ask, nine times out of ten on the days she plays, she's been at her mysterious computer since 7 A.M. Before she came to save my sanity, Eileen worked for top executives. We have no office hours, and she can wear shorts or go barefoot. While Carrie Beth was still in high school, because she worked for me. Mom was there most afternoons when her daughter came home. I think Eileen is happy working with me. In fact, I know she is; under that remarkable poise, her pleasure in what success I have, which she knows she's a part of, shows. She loves me. I love her. Even our politics agree, which helps her tolerate my radicalism. She is an exceptional human being, and sharing her openhearted friendship, along with her unique expertise in all she does, prods me into being my best—not as her employer but as her friend who wants, in all circumstances of our life together, for Eileen's life to be as good as she makes mine.

This gal makes almost everything I do possible and keeps me marveling that I managed at all before I could afford her full time. She not only handles the final work on my manu-scripts but takes care of all my business—pays my bills and the IRS. Unlike me, she understands what my accountant, bankers, lawyer, and financial adviser tried so patiently to explain to me for all the years before she came on the scene. She stays in touch with my agent, Lila, on contracts, copyrights, and permissions and even works right along with my literary attorney in New York. As the publication date of my latest book nears, Eileen is in constant touch with Ellen Archer, my lovable publicist at Doubleday. With Ellen's help from New York, Eileen carried most of the incredible load of Doubleday's arrangements that preceded

E. P. Day in May 1991. At the end of that day, she looked at me with what she could manage of a twinkle and asked, "Are *you sure* a promotion tour is more exhausting than this?" I count on her humor.

Not only does Eileen work magic at her computer on manuscripts, she *reads* the words, too, and watches my spelling. She's finally drilled it into my head that the word *occasional* has only one s and that cemetery is spelled with a final *e* and not an *a*. There is absolutely nothing she, Joyce, Nance, or Sarah Bell seems to enjoy more than laughing at me. With reason, oh, with reason. I am at my most vague, absentminded worst during the time I'm trying to live in two centuries. All four of them know this and make allowances. But more often than they know. I'm saved by their not trying to hide their laughter from me. I'm funny. They'd be artificial if they didn't laugh. A quite mild example of my vagueness is when I knock out a letter and then have Eileen clean it up for me. Two weeks later, she might say with that offhand smile that can light up my office, "Oh, by the way, I fixed the date on your letter to Dr. Richard Ottinger at Georgia Public Television. It was dated 1892."

Many of you already know that Eileen takes care of much of my mail. She does, with loving care. Some of you write, apologizing for adding to the daily mail stack. More than ever, now that I'm not doing any more store parties, your letters will assure me you're out there reading, but we do get swamped. I read everything you write, but I couldn't keep up the heavy writing schedule without her help. Except for Joyce, no one knows, as does Eileen, how much your ongoing devotion means to me.

At one point, before electronic security systems were available on St. Simons Island, Joyce and I hired a burly security man named Sam to drive around our house several times a night to keep watch. We grew fond of Sam and he took his duties of protecting us with serious dignity. He was not only trustworthy but could make us smile, often when he wasn't even trying. One evening, right after dark, Sam and his helper knocked on our back door. We had a guest, so Sam had seen a strange car parked in our driveway. " Just checking," he said, standing very straight, "because I wanted my new helper to know that wasn't one of your cars. I wanted him to know there are only two main ladies living in this house."

Now and then, Joyce and I still jokingly call each other "the main ladies." Certainly, another main lady in my St. Simons Support Group is Nancy Goshorn, who has been my close, comfortable friend since December 1968. She and her Aunt Mary Jane then lived in the house next door to Mother in my hometown of Charleston, West Virginia. Joyce had made a point of meeting Nance and Mary Jane on an earlier visit to Mother, but the enduring bond between Nance and me was reinforced in spring 1969, sometime near the end of a killingly long *New Moon Rising* promotion tour when I stopped off at Mother's, probably en route to Bebe Cole's Cokesbury store in Rich.mond, Virginia. Mother invited Nance to dinner and we were completely comfortable together. Of course, she had read some of my books. (Mother permitted few to get by without reading them.) I could tell Nancy was a true reader, but she'd had no professional or technical experience with books, to say nothing of research. Her work had been in the field of accounting and book-keeping.

Still, from chatting at dinner that night, I had one of my strong hunches that she would make a terrific research person. All my hunches don't materialize. That one did, and I'm still proud of myself for recognizing then that if we didn't live so far apart, she could be extremely helpful to me. Even in those long-ago days, occasionally I'd send her a difficult book I didn't have time to read and challenge her to summarize it for me. The expert way she did it made me still more certain that she was born to do historical research.

With Mother and Mary Jane both in heaven, approving, Nancy lives on St. Simons now, near Eileen. For as long as you, our readers, make it possible for me to go on writing, she will be handling the bulk of the research that used to take so much of my time and energy. Throughout the writing of *Stranger in Savannah* and *Bright Captivity*, Nancy labored—often launching off on her own ahead of even my awareness of what I might need—in the complex and detailed world of digging out facts, both historical and genealogical. One of my brightest joys these days is to watch her fine mind light up at the mere thought of peering at a microfilm all day long in some dusty archive. As Joyce keeps saying, "Nance has found her bliss!"

I honestly believe she has. I know I have, and it's good to be so sure about her. As I write these lines, she is in Savannah, again searching Couper documents for what she instinctively knows I will need: she is searching out dates, facts, national events, and Georgia happenings that may affect the daily lives of Anne and John Fraser when they return to St. Simons Island to live. Because she knows me, she knows I lack the patience for all this. She simply has sure instinct about what I might need, want to use, or discard.

Early in 1971, after my mother fell and broke not just her hip but her leg, Nancy moved into Mother's house to humor and care for her. She thus lived in two homes across a driveway from each other for years, being sure both Mother and Mary Jane had everything they needed—especially her love and patience. She always called Mother The Duchess, and with reason. But as she does with me (and I have a bit of the duchess in me, too), Nance knew how to be with my charming, opinionated mother—in love and real friendship. She knew when to be silent with her and when to laugh at her antics. I suppose, because Nancy and I went through so much together during Mother's last years, it isn't surprising that we work well together now on projects we both revel in doing. Especially when she was helping Joyce and me collect old photos of me all the way back to babyhood and high school graduation for an exhibit at our local historical society, we talked a lot about Mother. We talk often about Mother's unique way of encouraging us all to live up to our very best, about her seemingly impossible demands on us, of the charm she used so deftly to bring us around to her point of view. We also talk of how we loved her and of how she loved us.

In the final years of Mother's life, Nancy was her best friend. Their relationship not only made it possible for me to go on writing in Georgia, it relieved and delighted me. My much-adored father died at a relatively early age, leaving Mother alone, but not once did she make me feel that I should give up my life to come home to be with her. I'm sure you understand why her devotion to Nance (as Mother and I called her) still makes me grateful.

Now and then through those years, to give Nance a breather from the responsibility of both the ladies. I'd ask her to go with me on a promotion tour. She did the driving, stood beside me opening books and getting to know my readers (as both Joyce and Eileen have done countless times), and generally kept me calm and cared for. Because Joyce and Nance have always shared a special world, Joyce didn't have to worry about me while I was away.

I well remember one particular call I made to Mother just minutes after Nance and I rolled into our St. Simons driveway from a long tour. Joyce and Nance were in the living room laughing about something while I placed the call on the adjoining kitchen phone.

"Hello, darling," Mother said in her lilting voice, "I'm so glad you're home, but where's my Nance?"

It had, after all, been my book tour. I was her only daughter— her firstborn. She hadn't seen me in months. But there she was asking right off for Nance!

Nancy Goshorn helped me then just as surely as she helps me now with research and by meticulously keeping my lengthening announcement list. She takes the same responsibility for my needs as she did for Mother's. In all ways, I can count on her!

Where do I start with Sarah Bell Edmond, the other member of my absolutely essential St. Simons Support Group? With today, I guess: Before coming to work, she took her mother up the road to catch the boat to Sapelo Island, then stopped in her little red car to pick up our dry cleaning, a carton of my favorite brand of orange Juice, and the thin wheat bread Joyce and I like. My office is already dusted, waste baskets are emptied, beds are made, and swearing she honestly likes to iron (which Joyce and I find hard to believe), she's finishing our linens downstairs.

Sarah Bell calls Joyce "Miss Daisy" more often than she calls her Joyce, but she doesn't always pay attention to what Miss Daisy says. Our sheets don't need to be ironed, but they are, come what may. Of course, it isn't really necessary for Sarah Bell to pay much mind to Miss Daisy, since the two of them are permanently linked in a closeness seldom found between two persons anywhere. Generally, Sarah Bell plans her own work around our house, but if Miss Daisy needs something important, she won't need it long should Sarah Bell learn of it. They have lunch together. They phone and gab (despite the fact that they see each other here almost every day), and when they greet each other on Sarah Bell's arrival each morning (Miss Daisy is always at the door waiting), I know that at the moment of greeting I may just as well stop writing and wait for the happy, noisy explosion to die down. Sarah Bell's friendship with Miss Daisy is another source of happiness for me. Of course, I claim Sarah Bell Edmond as my friend, too, and she blessedly claims me, although my work inhibits her greatly in her own work schedule and I know it. Still, she is patient, inordinately wise, and sensitive to an almost uncanny degree to my needs as a writer.

I've heard her say to Joyce when she didn't think I was listening, "How does she write those big books day in and day out the way she does with us in the house? I have to dust her office and make her bed and there she sits tapping, tapping. Then one day, she hands me a big stack of pages and says, 'Sarah Bell, do you want to read the finished book?' Some days I think I can't wait to get my hands on those pages—can't wait to find out what she's been hatchin' all this time!"

I don't have a more perceptive, more involved reader anywhere than Sarah Bell Edmond. Sometimes I write to one of you, when you have written a particularly astute letter, to say it means more to me than almost anything when

I get response from a really perceptive reader. Actually, in Sarah Bell Edmond, I'm in contact almost every day of my life with such a reader who not only loves books but is mentally and emotionally equipped to bring her own contribution to whatever she reads, whether I write it or not.

Sarah Bell is from Sapelo Island, and that means prestige to anyone who has been around St. Simons as long as Joyce and I have. We are fairly sure that her ancestors once belonged to someone you'll also know about if you've read *Bright Captivity*—Thomas Spalding, who, along with John Couper of Cannon's Point, was a slave owner. Sarah Bell is objective, is highly intelligent, and believes Couper and Spalding did hate the ghastly institution. She even seems to understand the way they got around the issue. Some of my younger black friends don't, and I understand that, too. So does Sarah Bell. Even though younger by several years than I, she did live through drinking water from fountains marked Colored and not dar-ing to use a public rest room marked White. Sarah Bell is realistic, because if anyone ever knew her own identity, she does.

She is proud of who she is and what she does. I know of no one with more pride in her work—justifiably. Her sense of integrity and responsibility, her gorgeous sense of humor, go on endearing her to us and make her just what she is—an absolute necessity to the goodness of our lives, Miss Daisy's and mine. Another of Sarah Bell Edmond's virtues is her passion for baseball. She and Nance regularly replay every Atlanta Braves game, and I'm only sorry that Manager Bobby Cox can't hear their expert advice.

She is simply one of the greatest ladies I've ever known, who shows her thoroughly Christian (though far from stuffy) heart in all ways; by having reared two wonderful daughters alone; by never feeling sorry for herself; and by never once making me feel different because by accident her skin is a beautiful, rich brown and mine is a pasty white by comparison. No one includes Joyce and me in a more welcoming fashion than does Sarah Bell, who stands tall and strong and filled with good humor right alongside

Eileen, Nance, and Joyce in my St. Simons Support Group, creating so much of the peace and beauty and fun in the house we love and in our daily lives.

Where would I be without all four of these specialists in living? How could I keep writing? Would I even still be here without their separate but equal ways of helping me? Of loving me? Of believing in me?

Maybe I should simply ask, where else on the face o f the earth could I have assembled four such friends—except on St. Simons Island?

7

The Years of
Autographing
in Stores

et it be known far and wide—from me—that if an author is honest, he or she will tell you that booksellers are among the most important people in our professional world. Unstintingly, I thank this wonderful group of people who travel to book conventions, often at great financial sacrifice, who haul boxes of books and deal with multiple publishing houses for much of my own publishing success. It's usually the person in your local bookstore who hands you a copy of a new Eugenia Price title. For years, many of them have been hand selling my books to their customers or taking time to call and tell them that my latest title is in.

If I feel that way toward booksellers—as though between them and me stretches a strong, durable bond that holds us together—how must I feel about *you*, my readers, who have for so long spent your money and tried to forget your aching feet after standing in those long lines to get to my table so that I can greet you and scribble in your book? I love you for that. I love each of you who read me in Ohio and Kentucky and Virginia and Nebraska and Iowa and Illinois and Michigan and Wisconsin and California and Washington and Oregon and Florida, in both Carolinas and in Georgia and New York and Pennsylvania and Alaska and Hawaii and on and on through fifty states and all over the English-speaking world. I love you as a group of real friends, *sharing* friends, and whether we've met or not, I care about each of you as a person. I wouldn't take anything for all the times you have stood there, often holding my hand, always looking right at me, thanking me for the happy hours spent reading my books.

I will confess that I've had to work a little extra at match-ing some readers' enthusiasm when, time after time after time after time, someone has reached my signing table, face beam-ing, showing plainly that he or she has something really important to tell me. This, almost in the exact words, is what I've heard literally hundreds of times; "Do you know what we did? We went all the way to St. Simons Island and walked all over that beautiful churchyard—books in hand—and I'm sure we found every grave of each one of your people you've written about!"

You can surmise my ambivalence when someone adds, "Do you know, Ms. Price, my husband [or my family] and I moved to St. Simons to live, all because of your books!"

Ambivalence? Yes. I wish everyone in the world could live in this somehow mystically beautiful place, but we're overdeveloped now. When Joyce and I first found the Island back in 1961, the main north-south road, Frederica Road, was bordered on both sides by wildflowers and dense woods, trees overhung almost its entire length, and the road itself was far narrower than it is now. Four-laning may come and the remaining oaks will go.

Happy hours at autographing tables across the country have far outweighed the difficult ones, though, except that giving out and giving out—even to those one loves—can be exhausting. One famous author said to me years ago, "They'll take your blood if you go on being so nice to them." I'm entirely uncomfortable with that viewpoint and those of you who know how much I've enjoyed our times together will surely understand this chapter.

I'm doing my best to explain some of this because I've finally had to call a halt to autographing parties at all stores everywhere. On St. Simons too. This was not easy, but I did reach a firm decision about two years ago in the middle of a night spent in Jacksonville, Florida, near the beginning of the long tour in behalf of *Stranger in Savannah* and I need to tell you about it.

That night, about 1 or 2 A.M., I couldn't sleep. My good Eileen was, as she has been for the past several years, on tour with me, doing all the driving, handling interviews, finding our way to various stores and T V and radio stations, standing through each party opening books for me, placing our room service orders, spoiling me in general. She was, I hoped as I prowled about my hotel room, sound asleep in the adjoining room.

Eileen and I were due at a local Jacksonville television station at the unearthly hour of five-thirty the next morning, and I was still up, looking out the window at the well-lighted hotel parking lot where my white Buick LeSabre, named Mark Browning, was parked.

I have no idea how long I stood or sat by that window, but all of a sudden I asked myself, "Who's forcing you to keep on doing these long, exhausting autographing tours?"

The answer came at once: "Your readers and the book-sellers —those great booksellers who own or manage the stores where so many millions of your books have been almost lovingly sold."

Now, most of those bookstore owners or managers would have been surprised by that answer. No one was forcing me to do anything! Naturally, if there's a chance for an author's appearance, most stores hold parties, order a few hundred extra books, and generally do well. " If you'll come, Genie, I can pay my rent for six months!" The publisher is also eager for good-selling authors to get out there and help sell. After a quick bit of arithmetic, I realized that I'd been helping my various publishers and bookstores across the country since 1955, when *The Burden Is Light* was first published in hardcover by the Fleming H. Revell Company. I had been doing this for thirty-four years. Hadn't I earned the right to cut back or, better yet, to stop appearing in stores altogether? Even during those first moments of this tearing decision (and I was torn), I thought I had earned the right to do what I love most— write.

As I stood at the hotel room window that night, a new multibook deal was being negotiated by my agent, Lila Karpf, in New York. Lila had compiled in one folder the details of my lifelong sales record, figures that impressed me more than they impressed anyone else, because I'd been writing and traveling too steadily to have done much counting. My mail went on convincing me that year after year most of my books were being sold, were remaining in print because my readers talked about them with each other in state after state, in country after country.

Why not give myself a break in my remaining years by

concentrating only on writing? What I had in mind with the rapidly forming decision to stop chasing from city to city and store to store was not to become a recluse, not to stop answering my reader mail, not to climb into an ivory tower. I simply realized that I'd served my time on the circuit.

Would I miss the reader contact? I remember feeling almost ill when that question formed in my already weary mind. Of course I'd miss it! But I did feel weary, and I'd only signed a few thousand copies of stock for local stores, done one Island party, this time at my friend Debi Saeger's Shorebird Bookstore, and driven to Jacksonville. Oh, we had stopped even before we reached our hotel to sign several hundred advance orders for Ruth Schaul at Bookland in Regency Mall for her party coming up at noon that day—after the TV show at dawn. But the tour had just begun. There would be still another Jacksonville party with the fine people at White's after that, and then Savannah, where experience told us that super book-woman Esther Shaver would go on breaking records. Still, I was already weary. My age flashed through my mind—and the shocking thought that perhaps I no longer could count on fifteen or twenty more writing years!

In no time I realized that the tiredness was inside me: I had simply come to see that I had done enough autographing tours for enough years. It was time to stop. Eileen and I would be driving to Atlanta after Savannah, with an hour in Macon, Georgia, to sign a big stack of novels. Then on to the Atlanta area, where I would do what I fervently hoped would be a successful party at the Oxford Bookstore, then one at Cokesbury, another at the Office Sales and Services bookstore, still another at B. Dalton's, and one at Waldenbooks. The first would be at Oxford, well known for excellently planned parties; promotion director Lillian Yielding had already interviewed me for their Newsletter. (Because I'd gone to Rich's— book sections now closed— in Atlanta for so long, I admit I was a bit jittery about whether my loyal northern Georgia readers would find me in a different store, but I needn't have been.) From the Atlanta area we would drive up to Cartersville to a store called Chapter Two, which interested me because part of the locale for the Savannah Quartet was near Cartersville.

I'm not exactly sure where else we were headed. I only knew that at the very end of the tour we'd wind up flying to Cleveland, Ohio, where I would sign still more books and speak at a Book and Author Luncheon. *But my mind was made up.* After this tour, the time would have come for me to put down the lid. I slept for about an hour, then with far more energy than I expected, because the decision had been so freeing, I was ready that morning in Jacksonville for Eileen and the early TV show on Channel 4.

Before we'd reached the elevator to head down to the lobby, I had told her. "And just as soon as we're back from doing this show and have had our breakfast. I'm calling Doubleday. Dear heart, we're doing our very last autographing tour!"

Eileen has a marvelously calm way of receiving whatever shot of news I may fire at her. She is poised, knows me so well, handles me so skillfully, stands up to me in such a firmly gentle manner, keeps such a positive demeanor, I can't always judge her reactions to my eccentricities. I only know that she gave me a quizzical look as we stood alone together on that elevator, easing down to the hotel lobby to head for the parking lot I had watched over for so long during the night of decision.

Then she said, one hand lightly touching my arm. "You really mean that, don't you?"

"Yes."

"What do you think Doubleday will say when you tell them? What will Nancy Evans say? Will she agree? I know she loves you. You are your own boss, but what do you think Nancy will say?"

Of course. I'd thought about the call I'd have to make to my dear friend, the president of my publishing house, Nancy Evans, who through the final two volumes of my Savannah Quartet had begun to see to it personally that Doubleday published truly gorgeous books. Nancy had brought to the house, with the full support of CEO Alberto Vitale, also my friend, an entirely new aesthetic dimension to the quality and look of every new Doubleday publication. She and I had truly become friends. She is no longer president, but she was that morning.

I finished my room service breakfast more rapidly than usual once Eileen and I were back from the TV station. Knowing Nancy Evans reached her office early to find quiet time to work, I thanked Eileen for the second cup of coffee she'd just handed me and dialed Nancy's private number at Doubleday in New York.

"Genie, I'm so glad you called! Guess what? We've gone back to press for another printing. But wait, that isn't all. I've just heard that next Sunday you'll hit the *New York Times* bestseller list again!"

When we'd finished congratulating one another, I told her of my decision. If I live to be a hundred, I will never forget what Nancy said and the way she said it. There was a short silence, then in the same cheerful voice, she said,

"All right. You certainly have served your time on tour all these years. I expect dear Ed Waters will be disappointed, but we'll find other ways to let your readers know when the next book is ready. After this one trip, I promise you'll never have to do another promotion tour."

Ed Waters, my super southeastern sales rep, was due to join us in time for that day's Jacksonville Bookland party, and of course I knew he'd be let down. For all my years at Doubleday, I'd never been more secure and comfortable in a professional relationship than with Ed. He ranks right along with my beloved friend Bill Schoenburg, now retired from Harper-Collins. I knew Ed's children, knew and loved and had a special kind of fun with his attractive wife, Ruthie, whose life had also been spent in the big-time world of selling books. Ruthie would be joining my tour, too, at some point. Ruth, Ed, Eileen, and I had known more than a professional connection; we belonged together. We all loved one another, and I dreaded telling Ed for more reasons than that he is such an expert sales rep. Our friendship was so solid, I already knew he'd miss traveling with me as much as I'd miss him. In fact, I didn't expect Ed to let me off as easily as Nancy Evans had done. Nor did I expect quick consent from my creative publicist, Ellen Archer, who would be the one forced to think up new ways of announcing Eugenia Price books in the future.

If Eileen and I were to arrive at Bookland on schedule, there wasn't time for me to call anyone else. Except Joyce. I called her, and of course she was elated. She'd been telling me for years that after a long, tiring tour, I just sat staring into space for a month, losing precious writing time. Now, she admitted noticing that my end-of-tour exhaustion had increased with the years, even though I had cemented reader and bookstore friendships all over the country. In Joyce's typical light-hand-on-the-rein manner, she said, "Your readers are going to want what really frees you to keep on writing."

After Joyce and I hung up, I sat on the side of my almost unslept-in hotel bed and thought for a few minutes before dressing again for the Bookland party. Was Joyce right? Would the readers who had grown so accustomed to our meetings in stores (especially across the Southeast) truly understand? To my mind, there was no doubt whatever that I'd be able to write several more books if, when each was finished, I could rest and smell the flowers a while and not have to buy clothes, pack, and begin city hopping—ever again.

In the interim between that decision and now, I've adjusted somewhat to the realization that there will be no more happy conversations in bookstores with you, my readers—not even here on St. Simons Island. I do have to keep my friendships intact among booksellers everywhere. I dare not play favorites. My decision is firm, and I take solace from the reality of the bond formed through the years between us. We're still together in the same, close, good way.

You're still reading. My bookstore friends are still selling. I'm still writing.

8

The World of Publishing

ll is not glamour and bestseller lists and excitement in the so-called big-time world of publishing. Still, I have yet to think of an adequate way to show my gratitude to God and to so many people that I can earn a good living by writing books. I'm also grateful that writing is a profession from which no one has to retire until the old brain stops working. A painted bunting is calling outside my open door as I write these lines, and I've been thinking, between little morning exchanges with Joyce as we have our coffee, how absolutely wonderful it is to have a full day's work ahead of me, even though today is Saturday. The bunting flies off, chased by a wren shouting as though she's glad for me, too. It is even raining lightly, and to write through a rainy day is, for me, heaven on earth. In fact, heaven is going to have to go some to equal this. Of course, the aching muscles that go along with being past seventy are with me, and my writer's back, which I've had since my thirties, will begin to plague me soon. I'll know when it's time to stop later this afternoon because the muscles in the back of my neck—the ones that hurt like fury during a long autographing session—will let me know.

One of the reasons I miss touring with Ed Waters so much is that he always knew exactly how to relax those muscles with his big, strong fingers during an extralong signing session at one of those legendary autographing parties. He still calls me Mom (although I have yet to find a single streak of motherliness in me) because once during a seemingly endless afternoon at Rich's in Atlanta, when he was "punching" the back of my neck, a woman in line whispered to another, "I wonder if he's her son." I've received Mother's Day cards from Ed ever since.

The thought of my professional and heart association with Ed forces me to face the real difficulty of writing this chapter. It will not be easy to handle telling you of the wild, sudden, swinging changes that come and go for most people connected with the world of publishing, including authors. I want to write truthfully but without offense, because once one of these publishing upheavals is past and there is time for perspective, more often than not the problem cannot be placed on the desk of any one person. The entire corporate system has changed so drastically in recent years that my only means of coping has come from recognizing and eventually accepting the changes. Day in and day out, since the early 1970s, I have been working through these often chaotic vicissitudes.

I go on being amazed that so many people who love to read seem to know so little about what is really involved before a new book is in their hands, ready to be read. My life is so centered in all phases of publishing, I tend almost to forget that to most people, it's a foreign world. After all these years I'm sure I not only bore but confuse my acquaintances with publishing chatter; force them to make responses to me that make little or no sense to them. My friends are patient, though. For example, each morning before I start to write, I call the widow of our beloved Johnnie Wilson, who for years took wonderful care not only of our big yard but of our house and us, always working around my often erratic writing schedule. I still call Ruby Wilson every day because she is my friend, lives alone—and for Johnnie's sake. I can tell Ruby anything and often do. I might say, "Ruby, I'm packing to go up to Savannah to hide out for several days, because the copyedited manuscript came yesterday and I have to go over the whole thing and get it back to New York within ten days."

From Ruby's end of the wire, her rich, low voice—all understanding—comes back: "Oh, I know what you mean, darlin'!"

I know perfectly well that she doesn't know about copy-edited manuscript. Why should she know? She's a highly intelligent reader, but when would she ever have encountered a copyedited manuscript with all those mysterious markings and flags stuck along the margins filled with queries for me to figure out and handle?

This chapter is not about mechanics, though. It's about the big, general world of publishing as experienced from one author's vantage point. It has changed so drastically, from my first years as a published author until now, that my advanced age shows more quickly in conversation with a young person at a publishing house than in any other way I can think of. For instance, I mentioned to a bright, talented young woman who handles masses of complicated detail for me (much of it on computers, of course) that a book the length planned for this being past seventy are with me, and my writer's back, which I've had since my thirties, will begin to plague me soon. I'll know when it's time to stop later this afternoon because the muscles in the back of my neck—the ones that hurt like fury during a long autographing session—will let me know.

One of the reasons I miss touring with Ed Waters so much is that he always knew exactly how to relax those muscles with his big, strong fingers during an extralong signing session at one of those legendary autographing parties. He still calls me Mom (although I have yet to find a single streak of motherliness in me) because once during a seemingly endless afternoon at Rich's in Atlanta, when he was "punching" the back of my neck, a woman in line whispered to another, "I wonder if he's her son." I've received Mother's Day cards from Ed ever since.

The thought of my professional and heart association with Ed forces me to face the real difficulty of writing this chapter. It will not be easy to handle telling you of the wild, sudden, swinging changes that come and go for most people connected with the world of publishing, including authors. I want to write truthfully but without offense, because once one of these publishing upheavals is past and there is time for perspective, more often than not the problem cannot be placed on the desk of any one person. The entire corporate system has changed so drastically in recent years that my only means of coping has come from recognizing and eventually accepting the changes. Day in and day out, since the early 1970s, I have been working through these often chaotic vicissitudes.

I go on being amazed that so many people who love to read seem to know so little about what is really involved before a new book is in their hands, ready to be read. My life is so centered in all phases of publishing, I tend almost to forget that to most people, it's a foreign world.

After all these years I'm sure I not only bore but confuse my acquaintances with publishing chatter; force them to make responses to me that make little or no sense to them. My friends are patient, though. For example, each morning before I start to write, I call the widow of our beloved Johnnie Wilson, who for years took wonderful care not only of our big yard but of our house and us, always working around my often erratic writing schedule. I still call Ruby Wilson every day because she is my friend, lives alone—and for Johnnie's sake. I can tell Ruby anything and often do. I might say, "Ruby, I'm packing to go up to Savannah to hide out for several days, because the copyedited manuscript came yesterday and I have to go over the whole thing and get it back to New York within ten days."

From Ruby's end of the wire, her rich, low voice—all understanding—comes back; "Oh, I know what you mean, darlin'!"

I know perfectly well that she doesn't know about copy-edited manuscript. Why should she know? She's a highly intelligent reader, but when would she ever have encountered a copyedited manuscript with all those mysterious markings and flags stuck along the margins filled with queries for me to figure out and handle?

This chapter is not about mechanics, though. It's about the big, general world of publishing as experienced from one author's vantage point. It has changed so drastically, from my first years as a published author until now, that my advanced age shows more quickly in conversation with a young person at a publishing house than in any other way I can think of For instance, I mentioned to a bright, talented young woman who handles masses of complicated detail for me (much of it on computers, of course) that a book the length planned for this one would once have been priced at no more than $2.95— perhaps even $1.95. "You're kidding, Genie," she said. No, was not. I well remember that my first novel. *The Beloved Invader*, came out at $4.50 in hardcover! For the remainder of our conversation that day, I felt rather like a museum piece.

I'm certainly old enough to remember the days before computerized typesetting. Men (no women that I knew of) sat at huge keyboards and set type by hand. I even vividly remem-ber the days before copying machines, and I still wonder how we did without them. Our dear friend Elsie Goodwillie, who typed all my manuscripts when Joyce and I first found St. Simons Island, *cut stencils* on a typewriter for each page of *The Beloved Invader*, then made the number of copies Lippincott wanted by hand-cranking her old mimeograph machine! Elsie had too much humor to admit it, but of course she was a saint even to try such a horrendous job.

I also remember when Lippincott bought their first roomful of computers. You read correctly. The early ones were huge and filled rooms. Of course, I remember the foulup all over the publishing house the first time the computers "went down." I may say here that from the day those huge, bulky, balky early computers were installed, I could never again make sense of my royalty statements. Gobbledygook all the way. In the old days, at the J. B. Lippincott Company someone was *typing* out my royalty reports. Readably.

The innovations that have come about in the mechanics of making a book are undoubtedly all labor savers and vast improvements. What has changed in such dizzying fashion is the very structure of publishing firms. At least to most authors—certainly to this one—the changes, while probably unavoidable considering the direction of the world economy, are in the main not for the best. Mergers. Takeovers. Small, once privately owned houses now tiny parts of gigantic conglomerates.

All this has also caused huge, jolting, unfamiliar, frightening consequences for hundreds of people who work in publishing as well as for authors. The changes have brought some definite improvements but also some broken hearts, shattered lives, the necessity in many cases of finding an entirely new profession. I can tell you firsthand that some of these changes have brought downright grief akin to the grief that follows the death of a loved one. You see, the publishing business was once known worldwide as a "gentleman's business." For the most part, it was. In those days either publishing houses were family-owned, as were Lippincott and Doubleday, to cite only two, or there was shared ownership among friends who really loved literature. In my early days as a writer, most houses had not yet "gone public." There is no way I would dare try to explain the economics of all this, although I'm sure inflation is involved. When Lippincott published my first novel at only $4.50, they did so at a profit, of course. Publishing is a business. The United States runs on the profit system and I'm glad. Countries in which the free enterprise system operates, no matter their other faults, fare better. The Soviet Union's economic collapse would seem to prove that. We hear the phrase more often now, but our financial world has always run on "the bottom line," the bottom line being what is left over for profit after all costs are paid.

One thing I know is that you who have shown me so much love and loyalty through the years will see to it that my publisher's gamble on me isn't too great. Because of you, no company is going to lose money on me.

It is God's blessing that I am protected and guided in the always beyond-me realm of economics and book contracts by Lila Karpf, who is not only sharper than any tack but has a reputation in publishing for her integrity, her industry, her loyalty to her authors. And perhaps best of all, she knows me as a human being and has the grace to love me as I am: at times too trusting, at other times overly opinionated.

Lila and I still thank our mutual friend Faith Brunson, who back in 1981 made me realize my career was becoming more and more demanding, too complicated for me to handle alone. "Lila is in business for herself, so she can take on only a selected few authors," Faith said. "But she's experienced in all fields of publishing and you need an agent. You need Lila Karpf!" I certainly did.

Perhaps one of the clearest ways I can tell you of Lila's inestimable value to me is to say that this week, as I'm writing this book, she is reviewing all my old contracts, some of which date to the 1950s. What she is finding amazes even me. Her agent's commission is earned many times over, for more reasons than I could find words to explain, but if nothing else, she earns it because she can actually read and understand a publisher's contract. She not only understands what's printed on those long pages but quickly spots what is not printed there— for whatever reason. Too late now for me to deplore my own past naivete, so I won't.

But even though so many of you have liked my work all these years, take my word for it that I write better than I read contracts. Lila makes changes in my current contracts, marks them, sends them to me to check and sign, and I go on being amazed at how much I failed to notice without her. (I should emphasize here that Lila can take on no more authors, so please don't ask!)

Our friendship is deep and lasting and founded on the rock of our mutual faith in God. I sincerely hope that you, my readers, who share our faith, realize what a relief it is to me that Lila and I can speak of it freely and include Him in our decisions. Somehow I know this will make you glad for me. Happily, Lila has excellent rapport with my friend Steve Rubin, now the president and publisher of Doubleday. They respect each other, and I believe they both care about me as a human being.

My life as an author is rewarding and stimulating these days, but because of the bond between us, I want to tell you about a few of my world-of-publishing heartbreaks. I've had them. Right now I'm a happy Doubleday author, but there is no guarantee the present splendid circumstances won't change. Remember that one of Lila's favorite sayings, which has been elevated by me into a proverb, is that "one never knows from Friday to Monday who will be sitting where in the New York publishing world."

My first recent heartbreak had to do with Carolyn Blakemore, who has matured since we first met into an even more astute, skillful editor than our late, revered friend, Tay Hohoff, predicted. I will never forget my first glimpse of Carolyn, who is some fifteen years younger than I, enviably tall and statuesque. A long time ago, during a visit o f mine to New York, she walked into Tay's apartment wearing black slacks and a black sweater, hair in a golden-brown ponytail, with a birch log under each arm. I loved her on sight and felt even more devoted to Tay for having Carolyn waiting in the wings for me should the time come when I needed her to become my main editor.

The time did come. Tay left us, and I will always remember that during all of Tay's final, difficult days of illness, Carolyn and my equally dear publishing friend Richard Baltzell, both in New York, kept me posted on Tay's condition daily. Carolyn was even on hand to see that Tay ate at least something, because she dropped by Tay's apartment at the end o f every long day's work in her new office at Double-day. By then Carolyn had left Lippincott to become a senior editor at Doubleday. When Tay died, just as I reached about the halfway point in *Don Juan McQueen*, I felt more than bereft of the valued friendship of one of the greatest, most delightfully eccentric persons I'd ever known. I was also without an editor.

To complicate things still further, while I was carrying my grief over having lost both Tay and Carolyn, the great old house of Lippincott was suddenly no more. Except for its medical division, the long-respected firm, one of the oldest in the United States, had been gobbled up by a conglomerate, which had also taken over another famous old American house. Harper. Although I never understood the technicalities of the deal. Harper now owned Lippincott—and my contracts. Sometime later, my amenable interim editor at Harper, Peg Cameron, called me one morning in my motel room while I was doing research in St. Augustine for the next novel, *Maria*, and told me that because of the merger, nearly two hundred of my friends and helpers at Lippincott had just been fired.

My treasured fellow writer and pen pal, the late Gladys Taber, another of Tay's authors, had just written a line to me I will never forget: "Genie, I don't know my way any longer in publishing. I always felt so secure at Lippincott. But the sea is getting very deep out there!" It was, and although I missed Gladys's letters so much when she died shortly after, I took comfort that she and Tay were together again and that neither had to put up with the stormy, often violent changes beginning to happen in their beloved, once secure world of publishing.

I now had one goal in mind: to get to Carolyn at Doubleday. Not that I had my heart set then on publishing with Doubleday. I didn't. I was quite scared of the whole idea. Doubleday was so large, its list carried so many Big Names, that surely I'd be only a very small frog in that huge pond. But any author who says he or she does not need the objective advice of a fine editor is self-deceived or untruthful.

I must make it very plain here that I had nothing at all against the house of Harper then, nor do I have now. I greatly respect it. In fact, when I was a child, the school textbooks I always liked best were either Harper or Lippincott books. So, in a way, it was a youthful dream come true when, even though I hated losing my friends at Lippincott, I became a Harper author. I am still a Harper author. They not only own the hardcover publishing rights to all the St. Simons Trilogy and to *Maria* and *Margaret's Story*, HarperCollins, in fall 1991, brought out a handsome gift edition of another little book of mine called *Getting Through the Night*.

I am adjusting to the "deep sea" Gladys Taber referred to in the world of publishing. One can adjust eventually with belief that God's way—the way of love—need never be excluded from even the hard-nosed world of business.

Carolyn Blakemore, I knew, was the right editor for me and for the kind of writing I do. I am not what is known as a trendy writer. It is hard to put the books I write into any one simple marketing slot.

I did have to sell myself to everyone at Doubleday except Carolyn and my longtime friend in sales, Bebe Cole, who had believed in me since we met jn 1969 on that long *New Moon Rising* tour. To my relief, I believe we've all made it. In 1991, when Doubleday published *Bright Captivity*, the first printing ordered was well over 100,000 copies. But will you believe me when I tell you that all along my initial Doubleday autographing tour on behalf of *Savannah*, the first novel in the Savannah Quartet, we had to go back to press again and again—even before I reached home—because someone (who didn't know about my devotedly loyal readers) had placed an initial print order of only 7,500 copies? We laugh about that today, and first editions of *Savannah* sell now in secondhand bookstores for as much as $75 to $100 each. Why not? There aren't many of them around. Carolyn, with the inestimable help of Ed Waters, my Doubleday super southeastern sales rep, and Bebe Cole, began to convince their colleagues not only that I had a faithful following in you, my readers, but that you would probably put me back on the *New York Times* bestseller list. (My first novel to make the coveted list was *New Moon Rising*, the second of six novels I published before I signed my first Doubleday contract.)

Through *Savannah* and *To See Your Face Again* I really didn't know many Doubleday people beyond Carolyn and Bebe Cole. After long promotion tours together for those two books, o f course I knew Ed Waters. Dinners shared with Ed in one city or another, talk during the long drives together, had convinced me of the value of his expert advice, the joy of his ready humor, the pure pleasure of his company. With Ed, Bebe Cole, and Carolyn, I plugged along at building my peace of mind in a new publishing environment. About then the Bertelsmann Publishing Group, a West German conglomerate, bought the company, and I met our new president, Nancy Evans, at an elegant dinner party Carolyn and the house gave for me in New York just before the third novel in the Savannah Quartet went to the bindery. Meeting Nancy Evans changed everything for me! The same night I met her, I also came to know Bantam Doubleday Dell's new CEO, Alberto Vitale, whom I liked on sight as I liked Nancy Evans. Nancy, by the way, took over as president barely in time to see to it that, unlike *Savannah* and *To See Your Face Again*, *Before the Darkness Falls* had a better-sized, truly handsome design and binding. When it was time for us to publish *Stranger in Savannah*, this writer's shiniest dream came true: not only did Nancy publish the book, overseeing even the type design and every stroke of artwork herself, we both behaved like children in our mutual delight at the gorgeous look of the finished package. I was having real fun again.

Then, out of the blue came another heart-smashing blow. I once more lost Carolyn Blakemore as my editor. It did turn out to be fortuitous for Carolyn; because she is so respected, she's doing far, far better in all ways now as her own boss, working on an independent basis out of her New York apartment. But I was flattened at the time.

And about a year later, there was more. By then I should have been better prepared. But having always believed that publishing books should be fun—and to me having fun means deep, meaningful attachments to those with whom I work—I was certainly not prepared to learn that Nancy Evans, the symbol of that absolutely great time I was having, was no longer president of Doubleday.

Normally, such a sudden change in the very top brass of a big publishing house wouldn't so directly affect the daily life of a mere author, but I was knocked for a loop! One of my favorite sayings for years had been that when one turns sixty, total wisdom is given. "You certainly weren't very wise to have allowed yourself to become personally attached to those with whom you happen to work," someone told me. *Phooey.* I still say phooey. Remaining aloof and apart can have nothing whatever to do with wisdom. Love is always a gamble. Writing books is a gamble. Who can anticipate the public's reaction to a book? Who can withhold love for fear of being hurt when the giving of one's heart and self is so essential to us all?

Lila Karpf was the bearer of the stunning news that I had lost Nancy Evans. "I've heard," she said, trying to comfort me, "that Steve Rubin will be the new Doubleday president. He's a brilliant young man and he's been prominent with Bantam [also owned by the same huge German conglomerate]. Steve knows your work because Bantam is one of your main paper-back publishers, and he knows how important you are to the house."

Small comfort at the moment of realizing that my enthusiastic, spirited friend Nancy Evans and I would be doing no more beautiful books together.

"I'll just have to learn to grow up someday," I said to Joyce where I left the telephone after Lila's call. "Wanting to have an enjoyable time with my publishing friends may be out-of- date by now. Remember the old days when we could both form friendships in the business and count on them for years? I must be mighty unrealistic to keep believing that along with the hard work, it should be fun."

As usual, Joyce had no quick, pat answer for me. I flopped down in my favorite chair in our living room and noticed that she was looking at me in much the same concerned way she looks at me when she knows I am too tired, have worked too long, or am not feeling well. Finally, after one of her characteristic silences, she said very quietly, "You've had a lot of adjusting to do lately. Maybe there won't be any more for a long time." She didn't agree or disagree that I needed to grow up. She was too genuinely stunned herself. Joyce and Nancy Evans and Nancy's husband, Seymour, had also become good friends. Nancy and Seymour had visited us in our home. We'd been in theirs. Joyce is my friend. She cares about me inside. We share pain as well as politics and baseball and books and Bach and oddball humor. She was sharing my pain right then and it helped.

Finally, Joyce said, "Who knows? Maybe you and Steve Rubin will hit it off too."

"Yeah," I said. "Maybe we will. Certainly I don't intend to put the man behind the eight ball of my personal trauma. It's just that I've only known about this for a few minutes, and I already miss Nancy so much!"

I finally went to sleep that night with Lila's immortal line running through my mind: "One never knows from Friday to Monday . . . in the New York publishing world."

Days passed as days do. I kept working on *Bright Captivity*, the early chapters. Nancy Evans and Alberto Vitale had approved the deal for the new Georgia Trilogy. Nancy and I signed the contract right here at my desk when she and Seymour came down to celebrate it. I could not let myself forget that Nancy's name was on my copy of the best book contract I ever signed.

The passage of time does bring changes—a department of understatement if there ever was one. Do I miss Nancy Evans any less? If I'm honest, no, I don't. But far more than time has passed since she resigned from Doubleday, and much of it has brought a deeper, more lasting change in my mood, in the climate of my heart, than I could ever put into words. Steve Rubin, the intellectually keen, perceptive, altogether lovable person who took her place as president has been, is being, the key. I am again, despite lingering heartaches, having fun writing and publishing books. From the very early moments of Steve's first call to me when he took over as president of Doubleday, the two of us have leveled with each other. For that reason I will never forget his first call. I wonder if Steve remembers it half as well. (He does, of course, have many other authors besides Eugenia Price.) We have continued to share the same openness with each other, we both say exactly what we mean, and we trust each other. I believe in his frankness and integrity.

The world of publishing, in all its aspects, has always interested me, and I've spent time learning about it. I don't think I expect more than my potential as an author warrants. I know my limitations, but I also know the loyalty of you, my readers. Together, Steve and I talk about each step in the publication of each book. Of course, I think he's a fine publisher because most of the time he agrees with me. He even declared his faith in my judgment in a radio interview with my beloved friend Easter Straker, in Ohio. She sent a tape of it, and he's on record saying, "Genie Price is a pro all the way. I've never worked with any other author who knows more about all of publishing!"

There is no substitute for nearly forty years of publishing experience, but I admit that my long experience doesn't always keep me steady. It didn't when still another bolt from the blue turned my world upside down a short time after Steve and I established our friendship. You see, my telephone rang again one day, and it was my beloved Ed Waters telling me as gently as he could manage that Doubleday was reorganizing their sales force and that he had been let go. We weren't planning more promotion tours together, but I saw no way to manage either my writing hours or my emotions without knowing that Ed was out there keeping my friends in the bookstores all over the Southeast aware of what I was planning next.

I was still hard at work on *Bright Captivity* when Ed's call came. I went on, but every page I wrote for two whole days after his call had to be tossed out. Ed Waters had been with Doubleday for so long, it had simply never crossed my mind that I'd ever lose him. Ed's leaving, as events have shown, did not destroy me or my career, although the day I heard, I was sure it would. When I called Steve Rubin, I found him to be exactly as I'd believed him to be—totally understanding of my heartbreak at losing Ed, of my shock. Somehow he knew that my personal world had fallen apart. He has great business acumen and is careful of the bottom line, but he also knows there is more.

Through Steve, I was put in immediate touch with Michael Coe, whose already large territory had been made larger and who would now be my southeastern rep. He is a good one and the new system seems to be working, because there has been more response to *Bright Captivity* than to any other book I've written. And thanks to Steve's careful oversight, it is also one of the most beautifully published novels I've ever seen.

I can honestly say that it's been a long, long time since any publisher has (however subtly) tried to shaft me. But I have been shafted. Perhaps one of the indispensable aspects of grace is being able not to allow one disappointing relationship to spoil another. I did love Nancy Evans as a publisher and as a friend when we were working together. I still love her as my friend. I also love Steve Rubin as both my friend and my publisher. Am I tossing about the word love lightly? No. Both Nancy, much younger than I, and now Steve offer me the encouragement and enthusiasm and support any author needs. Ed and his wife, Ruthie, and I are still fast friends. Because I feel more involved in my work and safer with Carolyn Blakemore as my editor, Steve even arranges for me to have her expertise on a freelance basis. He is favoring me, I grant you, but being both sensitive and practical, he seems to see his authors as individuals with unique creative needs. Am I spoiled? Maybe, but in return I bring to a publisher the steady loyalty of you who read my work and show your faith in me by telling me that you are indeed out there, waiting for my next book. I also do my best to help the young people at the publishing house understand what *you like* in books. To help them understand what you, my readers, are really like, because as varied as you are and widely ranging in age and background, you go right on dumbfounding me with your devotion to what I try to do. Steve Rubin recognizes the value of this bond between you and me. In fact, I hope that reading this book will convince him that I believe he not only recognizes our bond but understands it.

Writing this little book, which some of you have already begun to call "our book," is giving me a special kind of fulfillment. For a long time I've thought you had a right to know something of what goes on behind the scenes in the world in which I live my life. You tell me in letters about your work, your families, your dreams, your heartaches. I also care deeply that you know about mine. I want you to see that I don't just sit down at my typewriter and wait for the muse to inspire me. Not only do my helpers on St. Simons work along with me for months and months before a manuscript is finished, but aside from Doubleday's hardworking sales reps, a separate support group takes over once the manuscript reaches New York: Naomi Fields, Steve's terrific secretary; Renee Zuckerbrot, sensitive editor in charge of this manuscript; blessed, cheerful Ellen Archer, my publicist; Marysarah Quinn, my designer; Whitney Cookman, my art director; Bebe Cole and the others in sales; and Jayne Schorn in the mysterious world of marketing. Steve also sees to it that for my novels I have the expert services of my longtime friend Janet Falcone, who is as superb as my copy editor as she is as my booster.

Yesterday, I had a letter from a reader who asked, "Could you take a minute to tell me the difference between your editor and your copy editor?" It honestly hadn't occurred to me that people might even wonder about that. The explanation is quite simple, really. My fiction editor, Carolyn Blakemore, reads the manuscript and does so-called line editing in order to check, first of all, the overall structure of the novel—how my characters do or do not develop the story and what balance I must achieve between story and the facts of history. No matter how long an author has been writing, this professional perspective is required.

Some years ago, while I was writing *To See Your Face Again*, the second novel in the Savannah Quartet, Carolyn had a chance really to do her thing with my character Natalie Browning. With one terse note in the margin, she brought me up short on young Natalie. I knew I had to write Natalie as spoiled, headstrong, hard to handle, but I went overboard. I wanted her to be a charmer, but a distinctly selfish charmer. At any rate, Carolyn's note did the trick; "Natalie is just too much! She's insufferable. I can't abide the brat. You'll have to do something to make me care one way or another what happens to her." Happily, it took only an eleven-page rewrite for me to soften Natalie's rough edges.

Thus, an editor handles style and content and pace and drama and believableness. A copy editor checks mechanical details such as spelling and punctuation, dates, ages, geographic facts. And yes, grammar. I loathe detail. Janet Falcone thrives on it. I write a lot more freely knowing that she will weed out my mistakes.

Both Janet and Carolyn have the kind of humor that allows me the freedom to point out, though, that they both are also fallible. Gene Greneker, one of our closest Island friends and a highly critical reader, caught us in an error so serious to anyone born in South Carolina as to be downright unforgiv-able. Carolyn missed it and so did Janet. So did Joyce and so did Eileen. In my novel *Savannah*, when President James Madison visited the city, John C. Calhoun came along in his party. Somehow, in my overloaded writer's mind the day I wrote that scene, I called John C. Calhoun not John but James! The sky didn't fall—quite—but I took pains, since I was still on tour and doing a lot of radio and TV and press interviews, to point out and make a joke of the horrendous mistake Gene Greneker had found. Because so few copies of *Savannah* had been printed in the first edition and the book had to go back to press so fast, it was months before the goof could be corrected. Not being an admirer of John C. Calhoun anyway, I rather enjoyed the whole thing. To add insult to the old boy's memory, two South Carolina historians had also checked that manuscript even before it reached Carolyn or Janet.

The world of book publishing today is often chaotic, unpredictable, riddled by painful changes such as those I've confided to you. It can also be rewarding. I've told you that, too. I enjoy it. I never tire of it. It's my world. It is not just the only world I know, it's the only one I want to know.

PART III

9

Now

Inwardly I'm not always the way I appear. No one is, but unless we're complaining neurotics, most of us, when asked how we are, say, "Fine."

Almost every day, *if* I'm free to work, I am fine, because much of the time I believe I've learned to live in the *now*. When Jesus said, "Sufficient unto the day is the evil thereof," He was not giving an order; He was merely being realistic. This very hour is what we have. Rephrased in the language of today. He was saying, "There is quite enough for you to handle now, so don't try to fix tomorrow today."

In my today, my *now.*, I have the usual aches and pains that come with my years and with which I've learned to live and keep on working. Why should I not have trouble-some muscles? (Exercise is such anathema to me. I'd rather ache than put myself through more than-the few minutes of calisthenics I manage each morning in order to limber up enough to write.) On the whole, my health is no particular problem, mainly because it is not an obsession. I've had high blood pressure most of my life. My doctor has it somewhat under control and wants regular visits but seems philosophical about me, in absentia, and goes on loving me as his friend. As do you who read my stuff. At seventy-five, I know your love nourishes and buoys me, keeps me going. Now and then, when our cheerful, dependable man-about-the place, Freddie Wright, has brought in the mail from our box at the far end of the lane, Joyce says, after I've shared a few letters with her, "You are so loved!"

She's right. Even though most of us have never met, still, we love. Is this the inevitable result of God's love for us all? I honestly can't think of another explanation. Do we even need one? We are told that "God is love," and if He is our native air, that's really all we need to know.

As I near the end of this small book, it may be time for a surprising confession—surprising even to me. It has been one of the hardest books I've ever written. I certainly did not expect it to be so difficult, but somehow I feel that I have not found a way to set down in strong enough words the whole truth of what your continuing devotion and loyalty mean to me.

If I share portions of a few reader letters, maybe you'll be able to put yourself in my place as I sit, near sundown, in my favorite chair in our living room, reading mail like this:

Dearest Eugenia Price,
I am a sixty-four-year-old retiree from Doubleday's Berryville, Virginia, manufacturing plant, where I spent thirty years. So I enjoyed the chance to get many of your wonderful books "hot off the press."

What a joy it was to read your autobiographical accounts, your own personal journey, and I can never thank you enough for the shining spirit I feel in you. I took a cousin to visit your Georgia Island and all the places you've made come alive for us. I also stood in reverence at the entrance to your house and longed to touch your hand to thank you for all the beautiful words you've given me—I hope you'll keep writing forever—I'll read every book!

For goodness' sake, tell me it's true that you're really writing a small book just about you, how you live your days, and what your readers mean to you!

I am eighteen and for two years my grandmother has hassled me just to try one of your novels. I finally read *Bright Captivity, and now I'm hooked, too.*

Words can never be adequate to thank you for the loving friendship I feel with you, although we've never met. There is something about the way you write that makes me feel sure that you are my friend!

Thank you for giving me a love for reading. In 1970, when I was just entering the seventh grade, a friend's grandmother handed me *New Moon Rising.* It looked so *long,* but of course I couldn't put it down! I have since read every book you've written, fiction and nonfiction. You opened the wonderful world of reading to me.

Thank you for being you—Eugenia Price, my friend.

As long as God allows, you will be a friend, a gift to someone, a moment of relaxation and joy, a comfort during the challenge of cancer (last year), an example of dedication and commitment, and a warm thought.

I feel as though we're friends, Eugenia, so could I ask you to thank your publisher, Doubleday, for having the good sense and taste to continue giving us books such as yours?

I've known for years that I'd be fed only frozen dinners each time you bring out a new novel. Well, dear lady, I thought it was time I let you know that my wife and I are, these days, reading your books aloud together and I am no longer fussing about not having a homecooked meal until we've finished.

My wonderful friend, Eugenia, I know I must sound like a slave driver, *but how long* will I have to wait for your next novel? I've just finished *Bright Captivity*, and at my age eighty-nine, you seem young at seventy-five! Please, please hurry the next one to me. I find I literally need to know how Anne and John fare in the years ahead.

I not only feel I know you, I know I love you! And I agree with your editor, Carolyn Blakemore, that *Bright Captivity* is your best novel to date! Being seventy-four, alone, and on Social Security, I can't travel anymore, but I transport myself with great books like yours.

My name is Tiny Nordlund and I just finished *Bright Captivity*. At age seventy-one, I suggest you take a short rest and then get on with the other two books! I can't wait. You are my very favorite author, and it's just as good to reread your novels as to read them the first time!

We drove across Tennessee to St. Simons last weekend to be on hand for the exciting Eugenia Price Day in Georgia. It was wonderful to have seen you at the big Book Festival last fall in Nashville and again on Your Day on St. Simons. Please thank your publisher for it! Oh, I do hope those of us who love you and your books so much don't irritate you with our adoration!

I am Jacqueline Thuma and I truly am excited about your plans for writing *Inside One Authors Heart*. Real tears well up when I think you care to pay tribute to your many faithful and loving readers (how like you!). I am already looking forward to the second book in the Georgia Trilogy. The first— thrilling! But I'll wait excitedly in the meantime for *Inside One Author's Heart*.

I have just finished reading the final book in your superb Savannah Quartet, *Stranger in Savannah*. I know there is a new one out, but there is so much to mull through in these four fine Savannah books, I find I must reread them all first. Even though we've never met, I do feel as though I truly know you, Eugenia, because you put your real self into your writing...

Yes, I do. Whatever my real self is, you who read my work and call me your friend have it. I want you to know, though, that my real self, like yours, can be torn by anxiety, stress, deadlines, grief, worry, and guilt. *Yes, guilt.* I try my best to keep short accounts with God. After all this time, I know when I've spoken sharply or created the wrong atmosphere around me for Joyce, Eileen, Nancy, Sarah Bell, Freddie Wright, and my other friends, including our faithful repair-men. Guilt is destructive, and so I do my best to make amends and ask forgiveness quickly. But until quite recently, I have carried about what I now see as false guilt, because my work schedule has grown too heavy for me to live the kind of neighborly life Joyce and I once lived on St. Simons; too hectic to write enough notes or to make local and long-distance calls that some days seem to need to include everyone.

Now, for the first time, I can honestly say that in the main, I have shed that guilt. I'm keenly aware that Joyce takes up the slack in my world of friendships, but I also owe a great debt of thanks to a Couper descendant, Jo Couper Cauthorn, to whom I dedicated *Bright Captivity*. One day, a few months ago, Jo and I were talking long-distance when, as I tend to do with her, I began to spill the guilt I felt for neglecting people. Jo and I are more than close friends. She did much of the ancient-Scottish research for me during the writing of her family's story in *Bright Captivity* and, in more ways than even I know, kept me going in the always difficult task of beginning a new series of novels. Jo, too, is a writer (a fine one!) and could therefore share each twist and turn of my often confusing mental journeys. She and Joyce have their own music-centered world of friendship, Jo and I have ours. Having her beside me in her singular, sophisticated, sensitive, blessedly far-out way is literally an anchor in my *now*.

Jo, to put it mildly, is definite. She is also deeply caring and, at times, startlingly insightful. As soon as I'd poured out my heart because of frustration over my neglect of those who think they have a right to expect my attention, she took off: "Drop it! We all feel real guilt about something, but this guilt of yours is false. You're just one woman. You've passed thirty-nine and you need to believe all the way down inside you that your main responsibility is not to a handful of people you happen to know and care for, *your responsibility is to your readers.*"

And then she told me about an incident she'd seen and heard in a Ft. Lauderdale bookstore just the day before we talked. Because Jo, even long-distance, has a way with a scene, she got through to me. She even made me "see" the crestfallen look on one certain customer's face when the salesperson told her my new novel wasn't yet in the stores. "It was a look that actually tore at my heart, Genie, because I could tell she was a lonely woman. I watched her count out her money ahead of time, and I knew she'd saved it up, only to be told she couldn't have what she so plainly needed— your new book! She even said she'd reread all your other novels, waiting for *Bright Captivity* to hit the stores. Your responsibility is to her."

Truth answers truth, and Jo reached me with the truth of what she was saying that day. I could hear her genuine concern for me and for that disappointed reader. Over and over again through the years, many of you have written in the very vein in which Jo was giving me her lecture. I also knew many of you do wait, almost seem to fidget, until the publisher and I can get the next book ready. I knew this, but until Jo articulated the direct connection between your loyalty to me and my false guilt over those people I thought I'd neglected, I was unable to free myself. No longer. Thanks to blessed, intelligent, convincing Jo Cauthorn, I am daily being freed of it. I love you, Jo. And as long as I have a *now*—even beyond my *now*—you will be in it.

A measure of success means an overflowing measure of requests; "Dear Miss Price, Please help me find an agent." "Please help me find a publisher." "I am a freshman in high school and you are my favorite author; could you send me material for my term paper by next week?"

Publishing friends write: "Dear Genie, I am sending galleys for a new novel we are doing this fall. Please let us have your comments for the jacket."

"Dear Ms. Price, My wife and I will be on St. Simons early next week and would be honored to take you to lunch." "I hope you don't mind, but we just drove right past your Private Road sign because we *had* to try to see your house!" "Dear Miss Price, On page so-and-so in such-and-such a book, you mention my family name. Could you please send me any genealogical material on them that you might have at hand?" Etc., etc., etc.

As Linda Ellerbee says, "And so it goes." But aside from my own St. Simons Support Group and blessed Jo Cauthorn, there is Tina—another essential friend in my *now* who truly compensates. She can ask me to help out in some way, can feel free to tell me her troubles, without taking one thing from me. I can tell her my concerns as well. Is this an art? I don't know. I only know that like Jo, Tina can tell me anything, ask me for anything, and never deplete me.

Tina McElroy Ansa has grown her way into the very texture of my life—of my *now*. Not only am I proud of her first published novel, *Baby of the Family* (New York: Harcourt Brace Jovanovich, 1989), I know of no other writer with a brighter, surer future. Tina is hard at work on her second, already contracted novel. I'm sure one of the reasons our friendship is so easy, so stimulating to me and never draining, is that she is the only other St. Simons Islander I know well enough to share the nearly unshareable world of a working novelist.

Tina is also a superb reviewer, much in demand. I fully understand why; *she thinks*. Of course, I love her reviewing because her scope of comprehension includes me. She knows about you. She knows our ties. Tina quickly recognizes what the literati call true art as she recognizes the value of my books written mainly for people to enjoy. Down their noses, I am considered by some critics a writer of merely "popular" books. Tina, who is an ever-growing person, convinces me that she reads my work in its true perspective. I pushed a button once long ago and began to write to please my readers, not only myself. It's fine with me that I'm a so-called popular writer. As Carolyn Blakemore jokes; "Don't feel bad because you keep getting on bestseller lists. Dickens would have been there, too, if there had been a list then." Tina understands this, and I love her balance, her lack of artistic prejudice. I fully expect her and Jo to write great books the literati will praise. In my now, though, Tina Ansa has come to be my kind of critic. I lean freely on her reactions not only to what I write, but to what I'm like as a person.

Especially do I rely on Tina's opinion of the authenticity of my black characters. She happens to be African-American—born into a middle-class, affectionate family much like my own—and really has no more idea of what it was like to be a black slave than I do. Still, she is so perceptive that if my black people ring true with her, it matters to me. Because she too is a novelist, my writing problems are no mystery to her. Like Jo, she is free to give to me. I am free to give to her.

In all our lives, if we're open to friendship, there are a rare few with whom we can be so natural, so at ease, that we can only be richer and fuller because of them. Never drained.

You who read my books have proved your devotion to me, not only as an author but as a person. Sometimes I wish I did, but I don't need to understand it. I simply accept with joy and give thanks. And I honestly believe that you who go on telling me you're waiting eagerly for the next book will be glad to know that my own now is rich and full.

10

The Future

What can I tell you about my future? What can you tell me about yours? Most of you know that I do believe in the ongoing life after these days on earth are ended, but as for our remaining days here, it has to be enough to say only that we will go on being loyal to one another, caring, our minds and hearts meeting in the books I write. Betty Lamberth, perhaps with a thought for my future, wrote this after I called for permission to use her name in an excerpt from another of her letters earlier in this book. In these lines you'll see that some of you out there do send me warnings:

> Your call certainly added excitement to our day—my husband, James's, and mine. Of course, you may use anything I write to you, but what my heart most wants to do is to tell you that, as excited as I am that you're

doing this extra book about you and your readers, I detected *tiredness* in your voice. As eager as we all are for you to write the little book about "us" and the next big novel in the Georgia Trilogy, we love you too much to have you fall ill from exhaustion! Please do us all a favor and slow down long enough for some rest. It is so important to me that you stay well and happy. I do love you.

I love you, too, Betty, but I honestly have no idea how to stop the one thing I love most to do. I know that anyone with high blood pressure should be cautious, and yet I don't want to live on this earth if I can't work. I have cut down on the number of hours I write. Most of the time I feel great, even though I know my obsession with work affects the quality of Joyce's life, of the life of others close to me. She vows it doesn't. I believe her because I want to, and just the thought of having a signed contract for at least two more novels is like a shot of adrenalin. I see to my own reading time, of course. Life is entirely whole for me when I'm either writing one of my own books or reading someone else's book.

Now and then I am sharply aware of my human mortality. I am repeatedly startled when I remember that I no longer can blithely count on ten or twenty more heavy writing years. I will be nearing eighty when the Georgia Trilogy is finished, but because it is so natural for me to fall into my pattern of wondering which series of novels I'll tackle next, I find myself still doing it.

I have enough self-knowledge to know that I work only because I love it so much and can't think of a single thing to do that I like half as well. Thoughts of it all ending are more painful these days, not because of my seventy-five years but because one of the friends dearest to me, Easter Straker, is right now literally battling for her life. I am so affected by what her days and nights—the moments alone with her own thoughts—must be like that I find it impossible to write more about it here. She has lived her earthly life centered in the radio and television work she loves above all else. No one has sustained and encouraged me more than Easter, and I want desperately to help her. I can't. But how does she face it? How would I?

Should the time come when I am able to work only an hour or so a day, I'll try hard to accept it, although now I'm not sure how. I do fear not being able to write at all. I'm not afraid of dying. Oh, I wonder about the moment of death. Who doesn't? But for those of you who haven't been with me in years, who might not see exactly the same God I now see, and who write to ask if my faith is still constant—yes, it is. You see, at the very moment I turned to Him all those years ago, I found that He had been forever turned *toward* me, that all anyone ever needs to learn about the nature of God can be learned in friendship with Christ. If you and I seem to identify with one another to an unusual degree, and I believe we do, it has to be because He is the Great Identifier.

With all my heart, I believe that He came to live among us on this earth because He knew that we need a real look at God's heart, at His intentions toward everyone. Being earth-bound, we need His identification with us so that we can truly believe He knows what it's like to be one of us.

Only God can identify wholly with everyone. Obviously I can't, or some reviewers and readers would not find my characters "dull, lifeless, blank as a sheet of paper." Those of you who do like my work prove that we all differ and how helpless we are to identify with people unlike ourselves. As a novelist, I have great trouble identifying with some of my characters, even though I'm sufficiently drawn to them to spend months and months of my own life trying to learn how and why they think and act as they do. (I have trouble identifying with some real, living people too!)

Many of you write of how well I understand the close ties within a large family. This would have made my mother laugh. Believe me, I had to learn how to identify with members of large families. I had only one brother, and our small family of four seemed replete in itself. We were definitely not "relative visitors"; we never dropped in on anyone and felt rather imposed upon when anyone dropped in on us. I know nothing of keeping track of cousins, and although my attractive nephews, nieces, and sister-in-law, Millie Price, keep fair track of me, we live totally different lives. We care deeply about one another but humanly share little beyond our valued, family sense of humor. I learned a lot about identification from my brother, Joe, who was district sales manager for Remington firearms. I dislike guns. He disliked books. But we loved each other. He was a rock-ribbed Republican. I'm a liberal Democrat, a real bleeding-heart radical to him. We argued over the National Rifle Association, which he loved and I deplore. But with God's help and a genuine, lifelong affection for each other, he boasted about my books (even though he didn't read them), and I sat still long enough now and then for him to show me his gun collection. From our distant worlds, *we loved enough to identify*.

Years ago I paid a wonderfully qualified and articulate reader in Pittsburgh to prepare for me an invaluable notebook, in which she shared a lifetime of professional knowledge about children from birth to age twelve. Believe me, that loose-leaf notebook is dog-eared from use! This greathearted reader is now in heaven, but I'd be in the soup without her continuing help in my learning to identify with parents and children. After one of my earlier novels, I well remember Tay Hohoff telling me what a dreadful mother I'd have made. "You get them born and then you never let them cry, you never change a diaper, you never feed them. They just lie there like dead things!"

You bet I'd have made a terrible mother, and thank heaven it's never been required of me. But I am a writer, and with the help of dear Kaethe Crawford's notebook, I can identify to a degree.

Another tough identification problem I have is to write convincingly about anyone's love of the military. I know gentle, peace-loving people do thrive on it; long to succeed in it; thrill to gun-bristling parades, the sound of drums, and the snap of flags. As a pacifist, I admit to real trouble here and yet I've had to learn to identify. Can you imagine how I struggled with the character of British Lieutenant John Fraser in *Bright Captivity*? I loved John as a person and he truly loved life in the Royal Marines. Joyce helped me a lot in understanding how John could be so tender, so gentle, and still bring himself to kill. In her youth she had known several fine, cultivated military men. Except for the young men with whom I corresponded in Vietnam and in my country's latest "adventure" in the Persian Gulf, I've never actually known a military person.

Of course. I've never been around a farm or a plantation either, and in the sequel to *Bright Captivity*, John Fraser is going to have to learn how to plant crops, which means

I will also have to learn to identify with the excitement of watching things grow.

For most of us, truly identifying is work, even when we belong to the Great Identifier. But no matter how different we are one from the other, a touch from His heart makes identification possible—*if* we're willing. I count on that. How I count on it!

The writing of this book has been an experience I'll never forget, and if I've been at all successful in convincing you who read it of my never-ending desire to identify with you, I have not wasted your time or mine. In your letters and in person, you tell me of your lives. You also reveal your hearts to me. As did reader Betty Lamberth, many of you identify with me, too. This is what matters. We may live in different worlds, hold wildly different attachments, beliefs, backgrounds—even different faiths—but what comes through to me is the content of your hearts.

At a recent symposium I was asked if, as do some writers, I have an icon—a quotation, a place to which I can go, something to grab on to when the tough writing days come. Without any hesitation I answered, "Yes! But my icons are visible only to me. On those days when I am so sure the current novel will never be between covers, the faces of two or three readers seen over the years at public functions seem to appear. I may not remember their names, the cities where we met—only that they are out there pulling for me and, best of all, waiting for me to finish another book. Those readers are my icons."

Most of us have never met, but we do plainly share a divine bond, and mysterious as it is, we somehow know each other. Whatever writing time I have left, I fully intend to go on beating away on this old manual Olympia, relying on Him, on my helpers, and on you who read—relying from deep down inside my heart.

EUGENIA PRICE

CPSIA information can be obtained
at www.ICGtesting.com
Printed in the USA
JSHW030345190821
17986JS00005B/84